D0495617

# CONTENTS

# PREFACE

Writing a book, whatever the subject, is always a laborious task for me. But writing this addition to the *Teach Yourself* series has been a real pleasure, because I am anxious to introduce as many as possible to the world of origami, which has given me so much enjoyment.

The main task has been to design the illustrations, because without them there could not be a book. Diagrams take a long time to prepare because, fold by fold, the three-dimensional paper model must be reduced to a two-dimensional drawing on a flat sheet of paper. And the drawing must be clear and accurate if the student is to understand how to produce the finished model from it.

It could be argued, I suppose, that origami has an end product that is not worth keeping. Nothing could be further from the truth. At the time of writing, I have a delightful collection of the world's best paper folds, carefully stored in transparent envelopes, which are in turn mounted on a sheet of black board. This way, they are ready to be produced and shown quickly – and they *are* produced and shown, at the slightest provocation!

If this art form captures you, as it has certainly captured me and many others, you will discover that it brings with it a new dimension in enjoyment, which is infinite in its variety and unrivalled in its capacity to make you relax and forget everything else.

Robert Harbin

# __ A SHORT HISTORY __
## OF ORIGAMI

'Origami' is a Japanese word which simply means 'paper-folding' and it was adopted first in English and then in other languages in recognition of the long tradition of the Japanese people for folding paper.

The Chinese invented paper, probably before the birth of Christ, and we can only guess that they were the first to fold paper. But we do know that by the twelfth century A.D. paper was used in Japan for folding ceremonial wrappers ('tsutsumi') for storage of household goods, such as herbs, and for gifts, especially gifts of flowers, where each kind of flower had its special wrapper. The present-day Japanese custom of attaching to gifts small tokens of folded paper called 'noshi' is a relic of this ceremonial paper-folding and there remain some other survivals.

Apart from occasional far-from-clear references to paper animals, birds and flowers, the earliest informative records we have of recreational, as opposed to ceremonial, paper-folding are two Japanese books the *Senbazuru Orikata* and the *Chushingura Orikata* both dating from 1797. The first describes how to fold connected groups and chains of paper cranes (very similar to the classic flapping bird on page 90) and the second shows how to fold a series of characters from a popular play. These paper dolls resemble somewhat Robert Harbin's Japanese Lady and Gentleman on pages 158 to 162. The folding in these two books is much more advanced

— 1 —

than the simple folds familiar to children round the world and it presupposes a long tradition of paper-folding in Japan before 1800.

The little paper dolls appear again in the *Kan no mado*, a manuscript encyclopedia believed to date from the middle of the nineteenth century. This contains several ceremonial folds and also some elaborately folded animals and insects which use extensive cutting: something which would not be acceptable today.

As modern creative origami avoids cutting it does not derive directly from the tradition of the *Kan no mado* and it is the flapping bird itself which lies at the heart of the modern development of the art. This remarkable folded toy was brought to Europe from Japan about 1880. Japanese stage magicians and also educationalists are believed to have been involved. The flapping bird was quickly absorbed into the small European repertoire of children's folds which already had a long tradition. European folds were, however, for the most part, restricted to a few simple hats, boxes and boats, together with the salt cellar (page 26) and what Robert Harbin called the 'multiform' series of folds (pages 73 to 83). Another multiform figure not included in this book is the curious 'hobby horse', which is known in Spain as the *pajarita*, meaning 'little bird'. The Spanish philosopher Miguel de Unanumo (1864–1936) took a delight in childish things, including paper-folding, and was fascinated by the pajarita. Later, by manipulating the bird base (pages 83–89), which was the foundation for the flapping bird, he created a series of somewhat angular birds and animals which nevertheless greatly extended the possibilities of paper-folding. His most significant discovery was the sideways twist of the flaps of the bird base which is also used in Yoshizawa's pigeon (page 93). A small group of followers of Unanumo came into being and the Praying Moor (page 99) is an example of their work. The Spanish tradition spread to South America and culminated in the vast analytical work of Dr. Solorzano Sagredo and the delicately creative work of his pupil, the late Ligia Montoya of Argentina, two of whose simpler models are the Tropical Birds on pages 129 to 133.

In Japan, Isao Honda made collections of traditional and modern origami and new books began to appear, notably those by Michio Uchiyama and his son Kosho Uchiyama. Then, quite independently of Unanumo, Akira Yoshizawa made similar discoveries about the possibilities of the bird base. Some of his work was published by Isao Honda in 1944. After the

Second World War, Yoshizawa began to publish his own books and articles and Japanese paper-folding entered a new period of creativity. Akira Yoshizawa's ingenuity is matched by his incomparable skill in bringing his models to life and he continues to dominate the art in Japan.

Before the war, paper-folding in English-speaking countries had been limited to the traditional children's folds, but in the 1950s it began to develop through the efforts of three people: Gershon Legman and Lillian Oppenheimer of the United States and Robert Harbin of Britain. Curiously none of them claimed to be a creative folder. Gershon Legman compiled a bibliography and also established contacts with both Akira Yoshizawa and Ligia Montoya. Lillian Oppenheimer publicised origami and founded the Origami Center of America in New York. She put folders in touch with one another and made many books available, including some in Spanish and Japanese. Robert Harbin demonstrated paper-folding on television for the first time in 1955, and in 1956 he published his excellent book *Paper Magic* which summarised the art and for a time became the standard manual in English.

The work of these three people brought together for the first time many people who had been folding paper for their own amusement in isolation and the newly available books inspired a generation of creative folders, especially in America where Fred Rohm, Neal Elias, Robert Neale, George Rhoads and Jack Skillman devised new techniques and basic folds which opened up possibilities for paper-folding undreamed of even in Japan. For a time the bird base and its related folds, the fish base and frog base, remained the foundations for folding but they were soon joined by more complex versions including multiple and 'blinzed' bird and frog bases. Before long entirely new ideas emerged including the 'box-folding' of Dr. Emanuel Mooser of Switzerland and 'box-pleating' developed especially by Neal Elias.

Despite the influence of Robert Harbin, paper-folding in Britain lagged behind until the British Origami Society was formed in 1967 from a group of folders whom Lillian Oppenheimer had put in touch with each other. The Society developed slowly but its membership grew following the original publication of *Teach Yourself Origami* in 1968. Since then the Society's magazine *British Origami* has become one of the world's leading journals on the subject.

In the 1970s, just when some began to think that the limits of folding had been reached, members of the British Origami Society broke new ground and produced a large number of greatly varied models of remarkable ingenuity, widely differing in style, sometimes mechanical, sometimes artistic. The classic bird and frog bases were now abandoned by creative folders and new, specialised bases were developed uniquely appropriate for the model to be folded.

The new Western techniques were taken back to Japan, where a younger generation of Japanese have combined the mechanical virtuosity of the West with the delicate artistry of the East. Dokvohtei Nakano and Yoshihide Momotani were two of the best-known among many new Japanese folders. Another Japanese, Shuzo Fujimoto, made new discoveries about the geometrical possibilities of folding, which he developed with great ingenuity. Many of his ideas await exploration by other folders.

In the 1980s Nakano's complex bases were further developed in the United States by John Montroll, Robert Lang, Stephen Weiss and Peter Engel and in Japan by Jun Maekawa. While their style was too technical for some people's tastes, their folding of anatomically correct insects and sea creatures, complete with all their legs and other appendages, finally proved that the possibilities of an uncut square of paper were limitless.

Contrasted with the 'technical school', the British Paul Jackson's minimalist style uses creases to tension the paper and create a kind of uncut paper-sculpture. Another Briton, John S. Smith, devised 'Pure-land' folding, which used only simple mountain and valley folds. It began as an attempt to find simple folds for children and handicapped people and ended as an intellectual exercise. Folding does not have to be complex to retain its beauty and fascination.

The 1980s showed the continuing vitality of paper-folding in other ways. 'Modular origami' (the linking of many identical folded units to form composite models) became popular and was exemplified by the immaculate work of Miss Tomoko Fuse of Japan. The First International Meeting of Origami Science and Technology was held at Ferrara in Italy in 1989, at which a distinguished gathering of scientists and mathematicians explored the awesome depths of origami geometry. There has also been a revived awareness of the value of paper-folding as a therapy for the disabled and handicapped and in child education, where it is employed not only as a manual exercise and for stimulation of geometrical awareness in the tradition of Friedrich Fröbel (1782–1852), the originator of the kindergarten, but also in less obvious fields such as the development of language ability and as an aid to conceptualisation.

The happiest thing about paper-folding is that it has grown as a truly international movement and folders in North and South America, Britain, France, Italy, Germany and many other countries are in regular contact and frequently travel long distances to visit the conventions of each other's societies. New discoveries are shared and exhibitions are held to which contributions are sent from all over the world. Groups have now been formed in eastern Europe and paper-folders from Russia have already visited England.

When we practise origami we pay tribute to the memory of Robert Harbin, the master stage-magician, who became so enthralled by the world contained in a mere square of paper that he decided to tell everyone about his discovery. He freely admitted that conjuring tricks depended on deception, but said that paper-folding really was magic. He would surely have been happy to watch the continuing growth of his 'paper-magic' and its spread to the far corners of the Earth. It was Robert Harbin's heartfelt wish that his beloved origami should ever continue to bring peace and friendship to all people and by sharing in that hope, paper-folders will honour his memory in the way that he himself would have cherished.

David Lister

Information on membership of the British Origami Society and about supplies of books and paper for folding can be obtained from:

The Secretary
The British Origami Society
253 Park Lane
Poynton
Stockport
Cheshire SK12 1RH

The Society has published a series of booklets of very varied aspects of folding, including the advanced work of some of the world's leading creative folders. There is also available for members a wide selection of books in English and other languages including Japanese. Write to the Secretary for information.

Residents of other countries may wish to get in touch with other paper-folding societies. Among them are:

The Friends of the Origami
    Center
71 West 77th Street
New York NY 10024-5192
USA

Mouvement Français des Plieurs
    du Papier (MFPP)
56 rue Coriolis
75012 Paris
France

Origami Societeit Nederland
    (OSN)
Postbus 35
9989 ZG Warffum
Nederlands

Belgische Nederlandse Origami
    Societeit (BNOS)
Postbus 100
B-2400 MOL
Belgium

Centro Diffusione Origami (CDO)
Casella Postale 225
40100 Bologna
Italy

Association Española de
    Papiroflexia
C/Pedro Teixeira No 9
Esc 1sq - 90 Dcha
28020 Madrid
Spain

Origami Deutschland
Postfach 1630
Mittlerer Graben 4
8050 Freising
Germany

The New Zealand Origami
    Society
79 Dunbar Road
Christchurch 3
New Zealand

# _ THE ESSENTIALS OF _ ORIGAMI

Most beginners are not able to follow diagrams and instructions easily and successfully, however carefully they may have been planned. As a rule, origami illustrators try to cram into each page as much information as possible. This practice is welcomed by the enthusiast and the expert, because it means that the book will be able to explain a large number of models. Unfortunately, though, a page filled with diagrams completely bewilders most beginners.

I have borne this in mind while preparing this book, and you will see that the earlier pages have been designed with no more than two or three diagrams on each page. All the diagrams are clearly drawn, and contain instructions and symbols to give you all possible help, and to explain the mainly standard models which bring you in touch with most of the Basic Folds.

A Basic Fold is a fold from which many models can be made. There are many Basic Folds, both ancient and modern, but this book will introduce you to just enough to give you a good groundwork on which to begin.

Look at the first fold illustrated in the book, and notice how the instructions are placed on the parts to be folded: FOLD THIS SIDE DOWN, and then TO HERE, and so on. The instructions are made to work for you. Later in the book, the instructions are placed next to the diagrams, and not on them, because it is assumed that by then you will have become familiar with the different processes.

Always fold carefully, accurately and neatly. If you fold carelessly, the result will be disastrous.

Study each diagram showing the complete folded model, and only then, place your origami paper in front of you and make your first fold.

When you make a fold, always crease the paper firmly with the back of your thumbnail. Good creases make folding easy, and are an invaluable guide later in the model, when you are making a series of folds.

Pre-creasing is an important feature. Consider, for example, the Japanese Lady (page 161). This model was sent to Samuel Randlett, who immediately used the idea to produce his fine Fish (page 163). Notice how he pre-creases the paper he uses so that everything folds into place at the right moment.

Before you make a Reverse Fold, pre-crease the paper by folding the whole thickness before opening the paper and making the fold (see Reverse Folds).

Notice how paper coloured on one side is used to get the maximum effect for each model. The subject of paper is an important one. Origami paper should be strong, thin and suitably coloured. But if you cannot find special origami paper, almost any paper may be used.

If you are instructed to use a square of paper, make sure that it really is square, and that a rectangle is a true rectangle. Most of the models in this book are based on squares of paper, but there is no regular rule about this, as all shapes of paper can be used, according to the model's needs. See, for example, the Ornithonimus (page 167) and Aladdin's Lamp (page 170).

Origami is not a simple art. To the expert, it is a challenge to the eye, the brain and the fingers – a wonderful mental and physical therapy.

When you fold one of the decorations explained in this book, you will find that by altering this or that fold you can invent endless shapes. In fact, you can improvise for hours.

When you have mastered the Basic Folds, you will then be equipped to produce figures and shapes of your own inventions. Have something in mind, and then consider the best Base from which to start. You will notice that there are three different ways in which to make a penguin. The penguin seems to be a favourite subject, and almost every folder has a go at it.

Watch out for terms like Squash Fold. It is so named because you do just that – squash the part indicated so that the sides bulge and it flattens, in most cases symmetrically.

Study the Petal Folds, the Rabbit's Ears and the various Bases, and try to remember what they are. If you get stuck, have a look at the Contents and refer to the pages concerned.

You will notice that certain procedures are used over and over again. You will soon get used to these and be able to carry them out automatically.

When you have folded everything in the first half of the book, you will find that more and more diagrams begin to appear on each page, and that the symbols begin to play a bigger part than the instructions. Decoration 2 (page 153) has been included as an exercise so try to make this up using the symbols only.

Finally – take it slowly; fold carefully, neatly and accurately. And START AT THE BEGINNING!

## ———————— A note on symbols ————————

The symbols used in this book are based on Akira Yoshizawa's code of lines and arrows. Symbols will become second nature to you when folding as they are easy to acquire.

The moment you see a line of dashes, you know that the paper must be Valley Folded along that line. When you see a line of dashes and dots, you recognise the sign for a Mountain Fold. To make a Mountain Fold, you naturally turn the paper upside down and make a Valley Fold.

Arrows show the directions in which you must fold: left, right, up, down, in front, behind and into.

You will notice one arrow which shows that a drawing has been enlarged for clarity. Another arrow indicates that a model must be opened out (see Samuel Randlett's Fish, page 163). My own little black arrow indicates that you must sink, press, squeeze or push in at certain points.

The symbols are in fact self-explanatory. They are simple common sense, and can be learnt in about ten minutes.

Try to use the symbols only and ignore explanations. This will help you when you come to read Japanese origami books.

*Valley fold*
A series of dashes

means fold
like this.

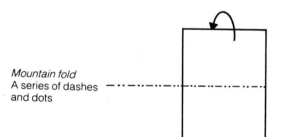

*Mountain fold*
A series of dashes
and dots

means fold
like this.

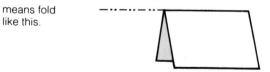

If a drawing
was marked
with these symbols

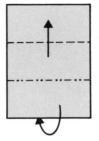

the result
should be
this.

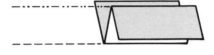

When a drawing
is followed by
this little looped
arrow

turn the
model over
so.

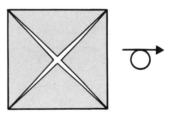

This black arrow

means push in.

Thin lines mean creases.

This symbol

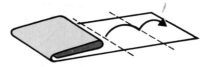

means

fold over and
over.

# MAKE THIS WATER BOMB BASE AND PRELIMINARY FOLD

If a drawing is
marked like this

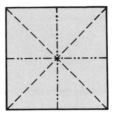

you make this
water bomb base.

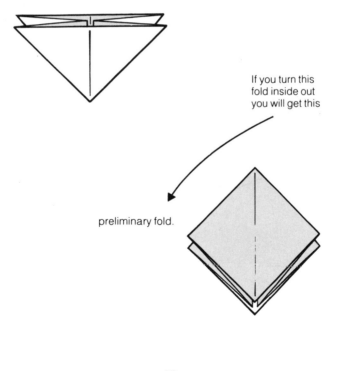

If you turn this
fold inside out
you will get this

preliminary fold.

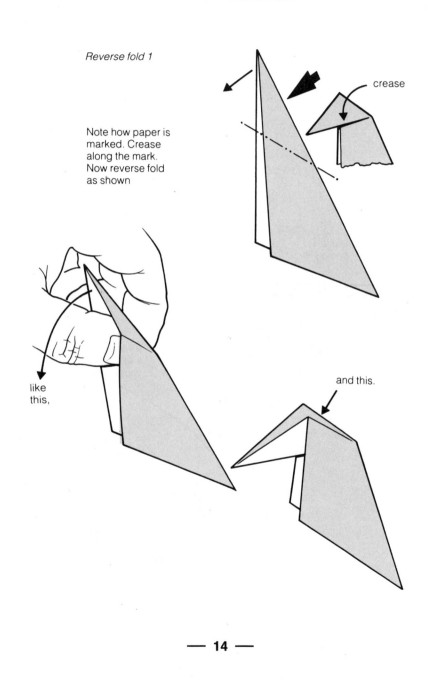

Reverse fold 1

Note how paper is
marked. Crease
along the mark.
Now reverse fold
as shown

crease

like
this,

and this.

*Reverse fold 2*

Note how paper is
marked. Crease
along the mark.
Now reverse fold
as shown.

crease

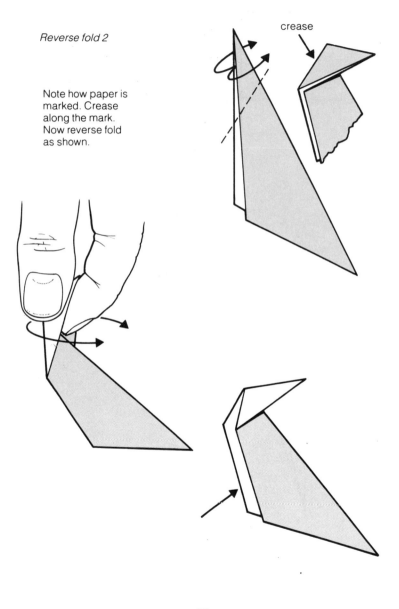

1

How to fold feet
(birds, animals, people).
1 Reverse fold 2.
2 Reverse fold 1.
3 Two reverse folds.

2

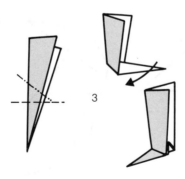

3

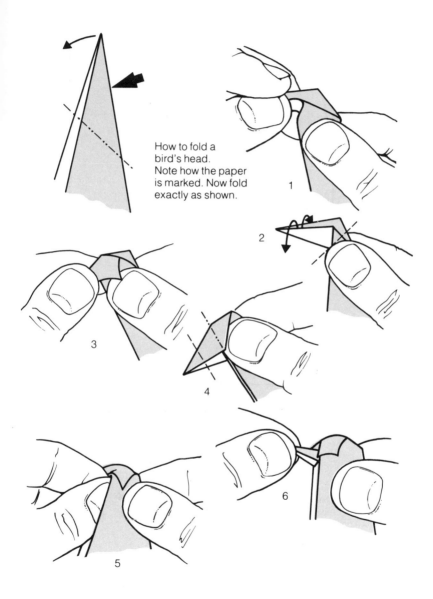

How to fold a
bird's head.
Note how the paper
is marked. Now fold
exactly as shown.

1

2

3

4

5

6

Start with the white side of the paper facing you.

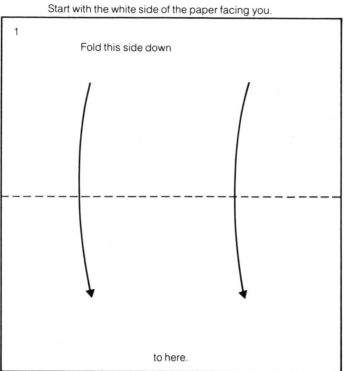

1

Fold this side down

to here.

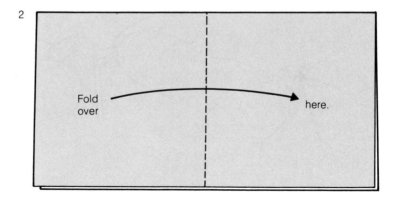

2

Fold
over

here.

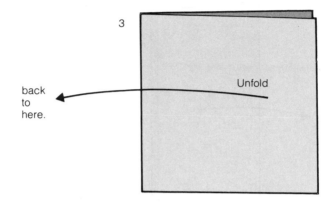

3

back
to
here.

Unfold

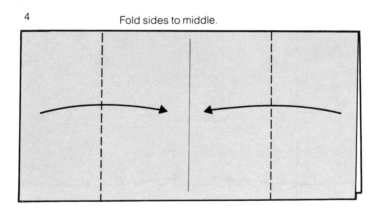

4          Fold sides to middle.

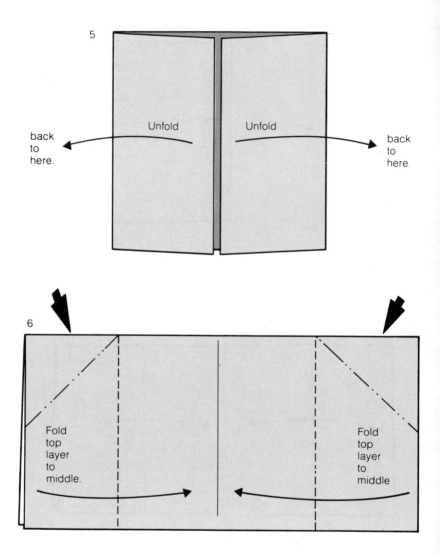

5

Unfold     Unfold

back
to
here.

back
to
here.

6

Fold
top
layer
to
middle.

Fold
top
layer
to
middle

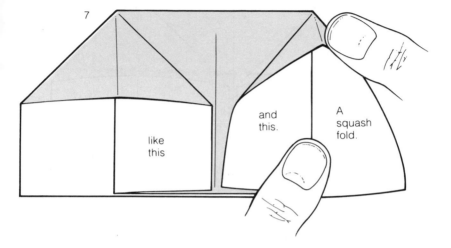

7 like this

and this.

A squash fold.

Now draw doors and windows.

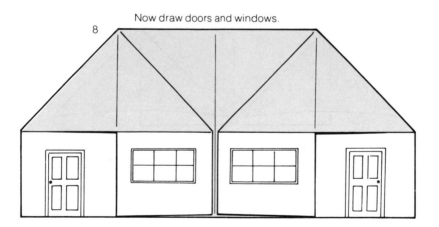

8

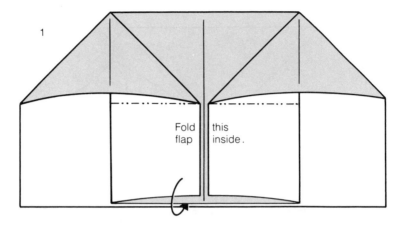

1

Fold | this
flap | inside.

Now—
turn the
model over

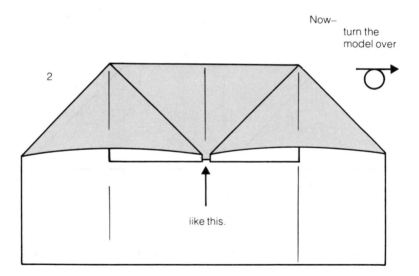

2

iike this.

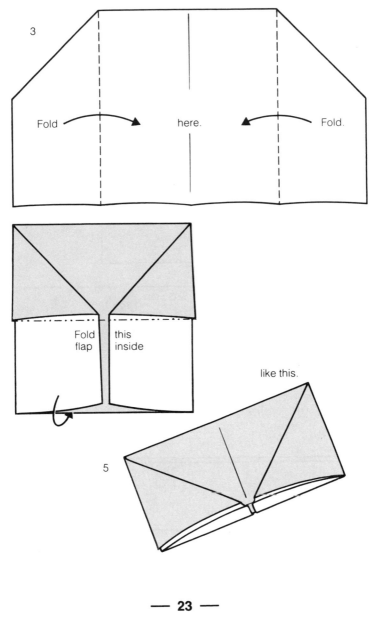

3

Fold → here. ← Fold.

4

Fold this
flap inside

like this.

5

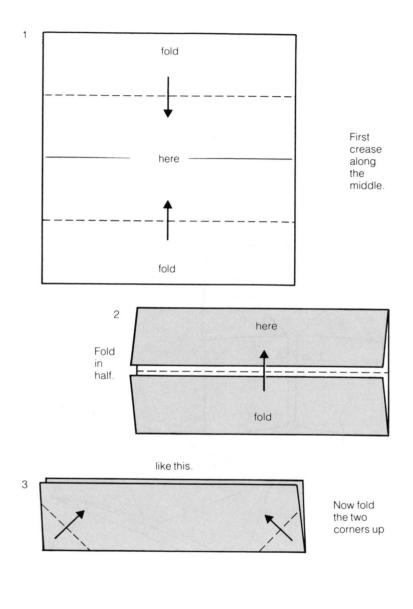

1

fold

↓

here

↑

fold

First
crease
along
the
middle.

2

here

↑

Fold
in
half.

fold

like this.

3

Now fold
the two
corners up

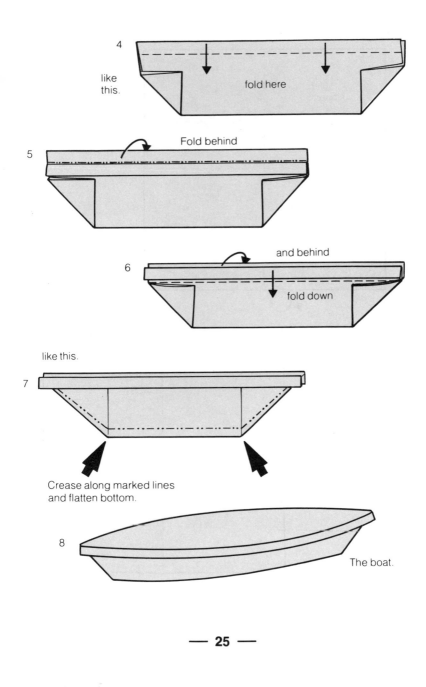

4
like
this.
fold here

Fold behind
5

and behind
6
fold down

like this.
7

Crease along marked lines
and flatten bottom.

8
The boat.

1

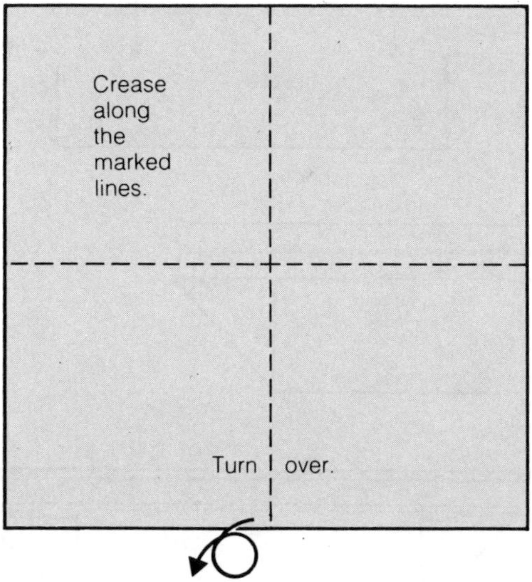

Crease
along
the
marked
lines.

Turn over.

2

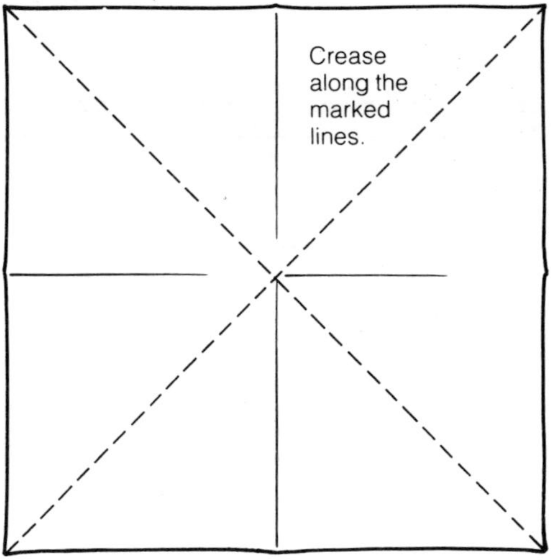

Crease
along the
marked
lines.

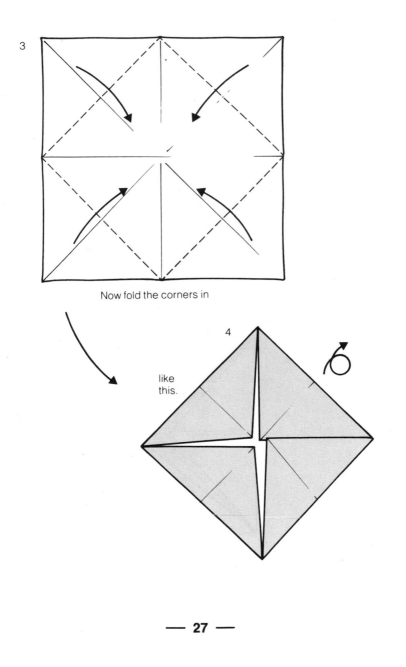

3

Now fold the corners in

4

like
this.

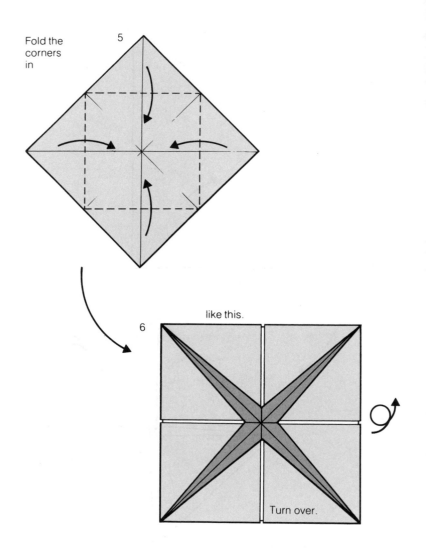

Fold the
corners
in

5

like this.

6

Turn over.

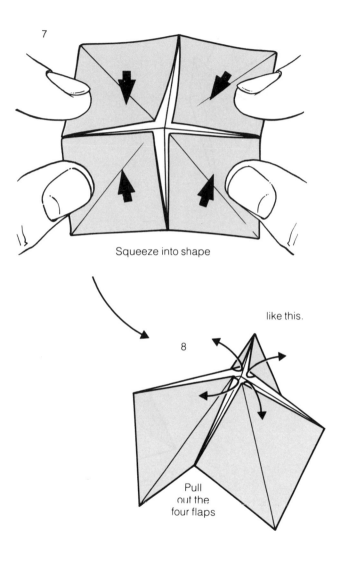

7

Squeeze into shape

like this.

8

Pull
out the
four flaps

9    like this.

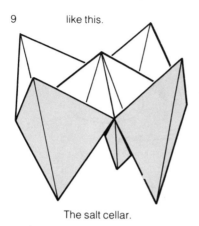

The salt cellar.

10

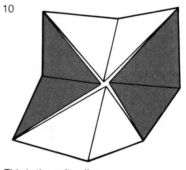

This is the salt cellar
upside down. Colour
the areas shown

11

to make
the colour
changer.

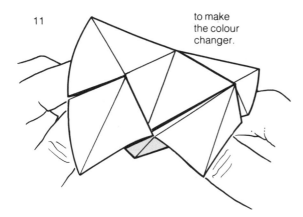

And this
shows how you
make it work.

12

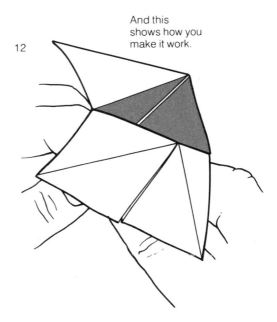

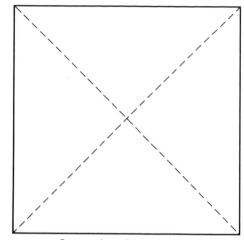

Crease along the marked lines.

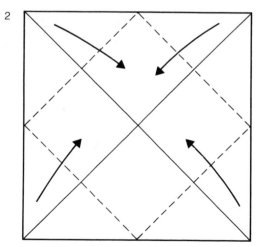

Fold the four corners to the centre.

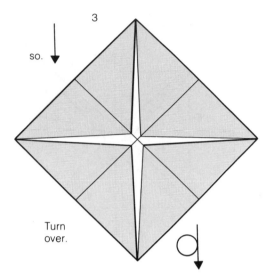

3

so.

Turn
over.

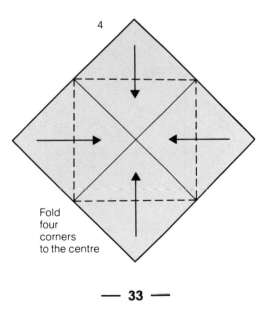

4

Fold
four
corners
to the centre

enlarged
view

5

fold
up

fold
left

fold
down

so.

fold
right

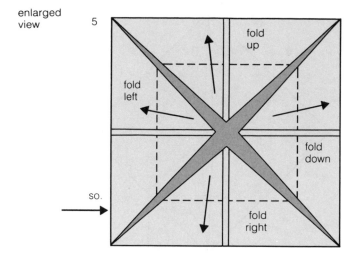

6

Turn over.

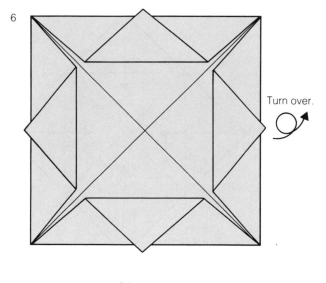

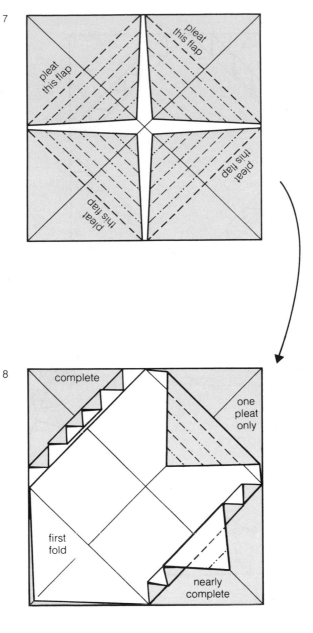

7

pleat
this flap

pleat
this flap

pleat
this flap

pleat
this flap

8

complete

one
pleat
only

first
fold

nearly
complete

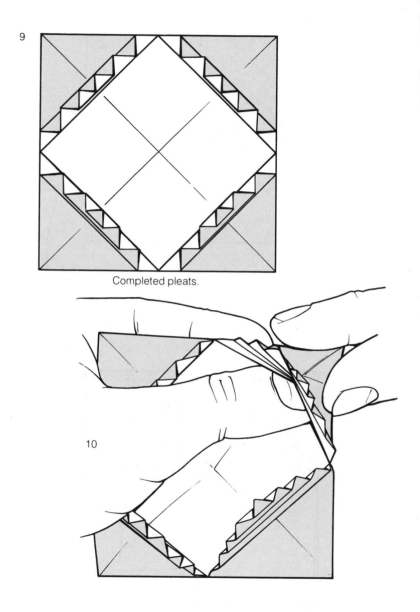

Completed pleats.

Push left thumb into each
corner and press together
on the outside until the
fancy box is completed.

so.

11

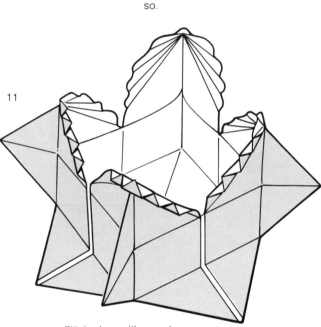

Fill the box with sweets.

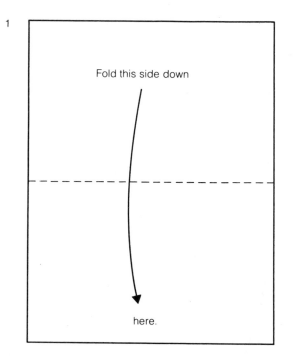

1

Fold this side down

here.

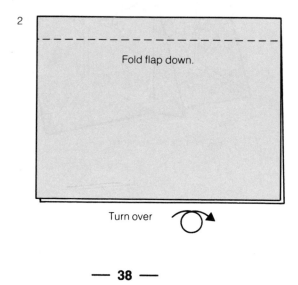

2

Fold flap down.

Turn over

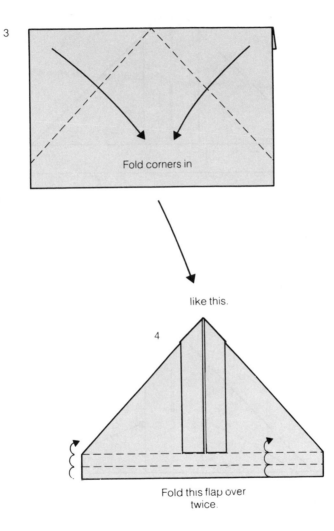

3

Fold corners in

like this.

4

Fold this flap over
twice.

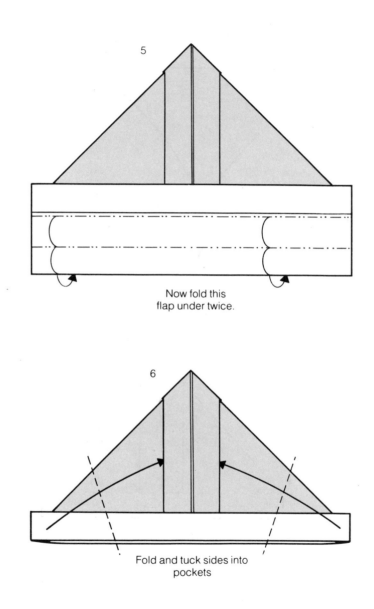

5

Now fold this
flap under twice.

6

Fold and tuck sides into
pockets

7

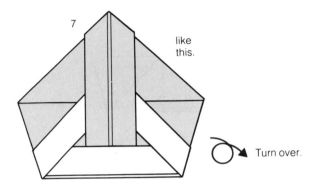

like
this.

Turn over.

8

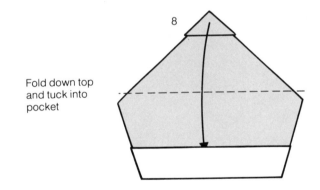

Fold down top
and tuck into
pocket

9     like this.

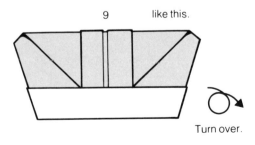

Turn over.

10

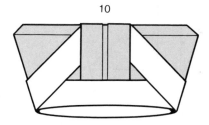

The turban complete.

Try this with
a sheet of
newspaper.

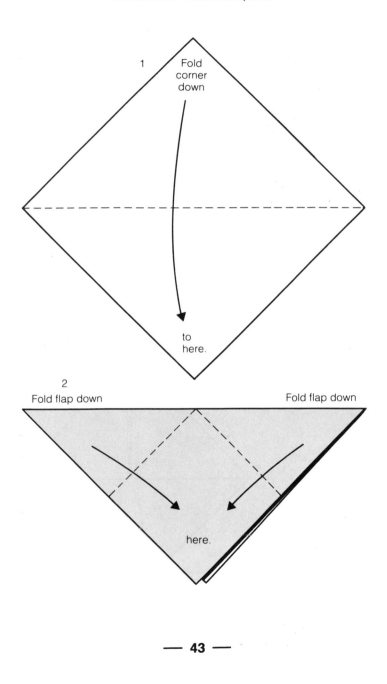

1   Fold
    corner
    down

to
here.

2
Fold flap down                          Fold flap down

here.

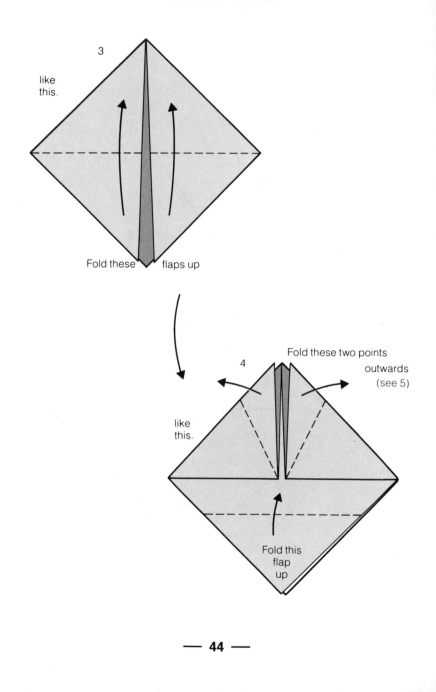

3

like
this.

Fold these flaps up

Fold these two points

outwards
(see 5)

4

like
this.

Fold this
flap
up

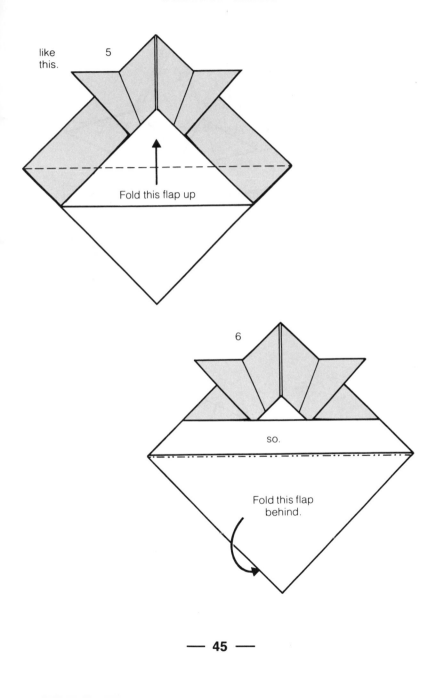

like
this.

5

Fold this flap up

6

so.

Fold this flap
behind.

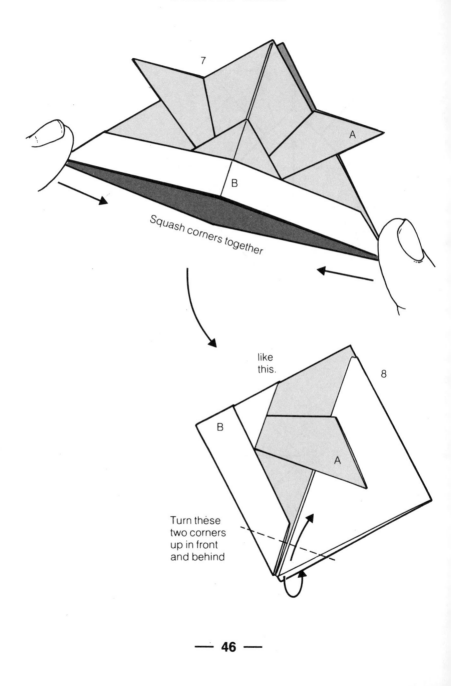

7

A

B

Squash corners together

like
this.

8

B

A

Turn these
two corners
up in front
and behind

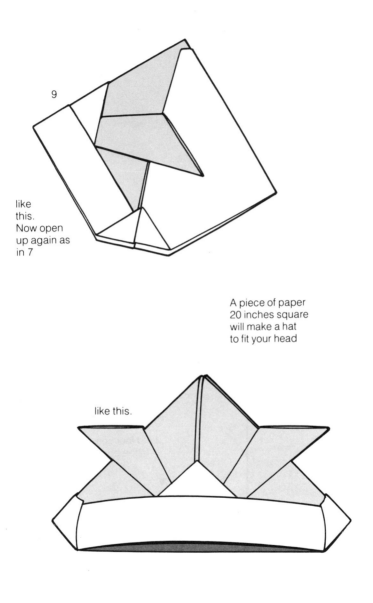

9

like
this.
Now open
up again as
in 7

A piece of paper
20 inches square
will make a hat
to fit your head

like this.

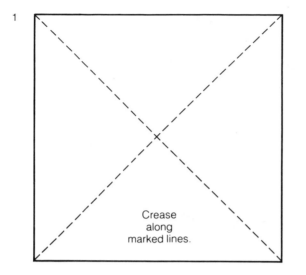

1

Crease
along
marked lines.

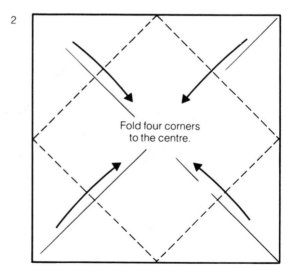

2

Fold four corners
to the centre.

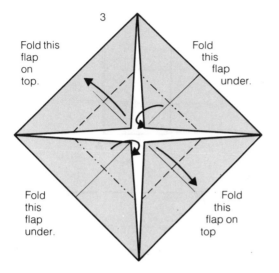

3

Fold this flap on top.

Fold this flap under.

Fold this flap under.

Fold this flap on top

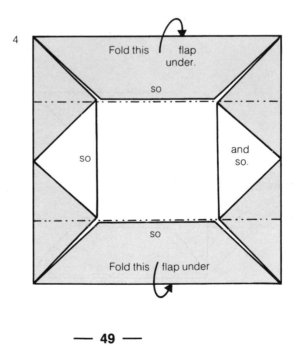

4

Fold this flap under.

so

so

and so.

so

Fold this flap under

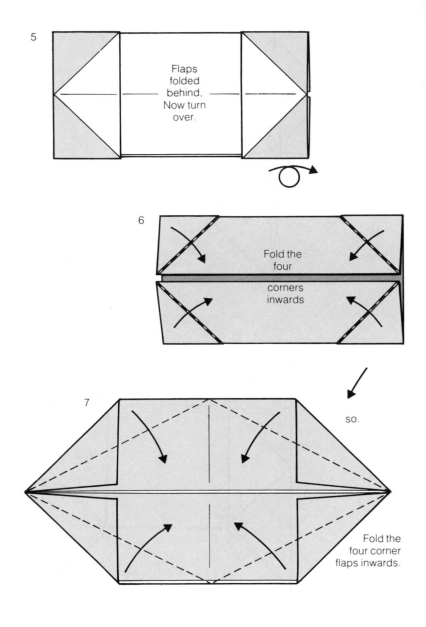

5

Flaps
folded
behind,
Now turn
over.

6

Fold the
four

corners
inwards

so.

7

Fold the
four corner
flaps inwards.

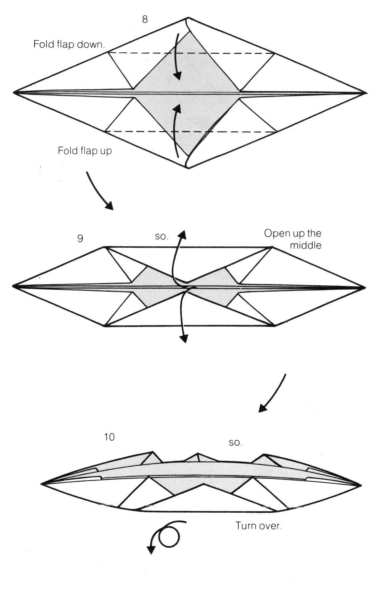

8

Fold flap down.

Fold flap up

9    so.    Open up the middle

10    so.

Turn over.

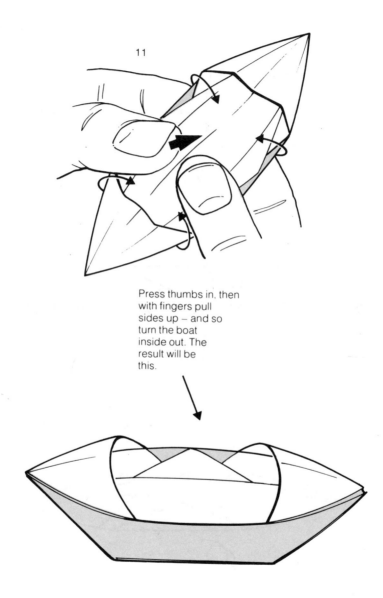

11

Press thumbs in, then
with fingers pull
sides up – and so
turn the boat
inside out. The
result will be
this.

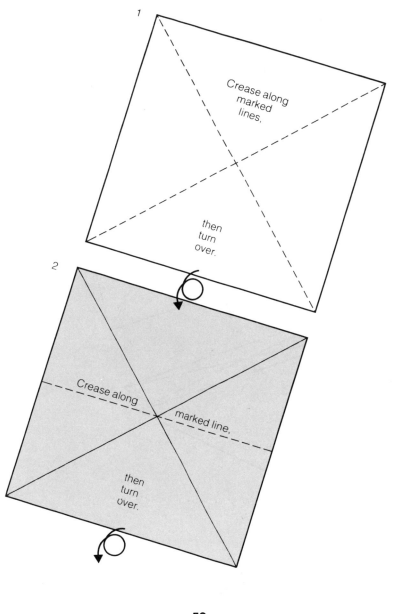

1

Crease along
marked
lines,

then
turn
over.

2

Crease along

marked line,

then
turn
over.

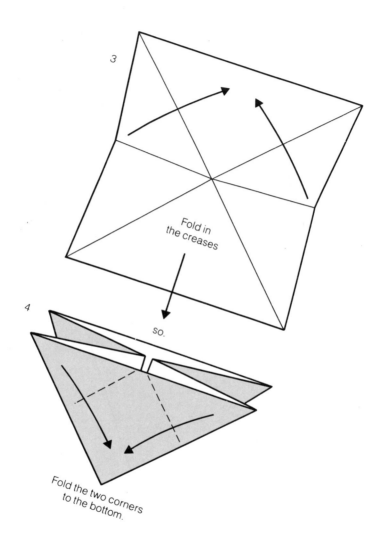

3

Fold in
the creases

so.

4

Fold the two corners
to the bottom.

5

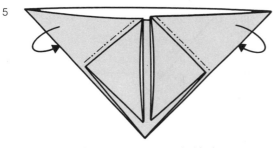

Fold the two corners behind.

6

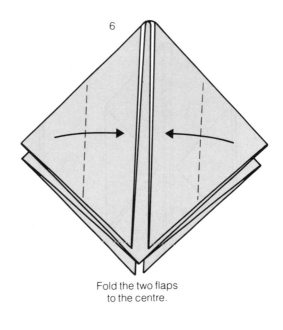

Fold the two flaps
to the centre.

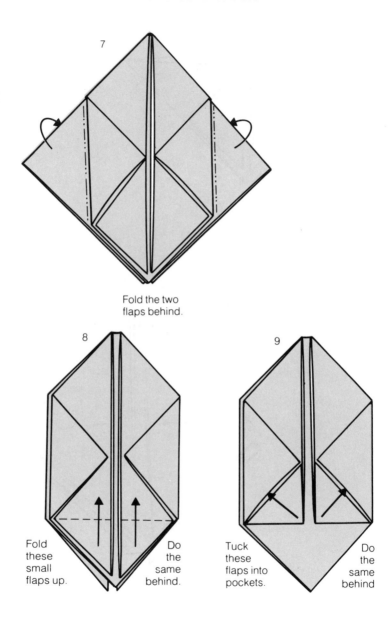

7

Fold the two
flaps behind.

8

Fold
these
small
flaps up.

Do
the
same
behind.

9

Tuck
these
flaps into
pockets.

Do
the
same
behind

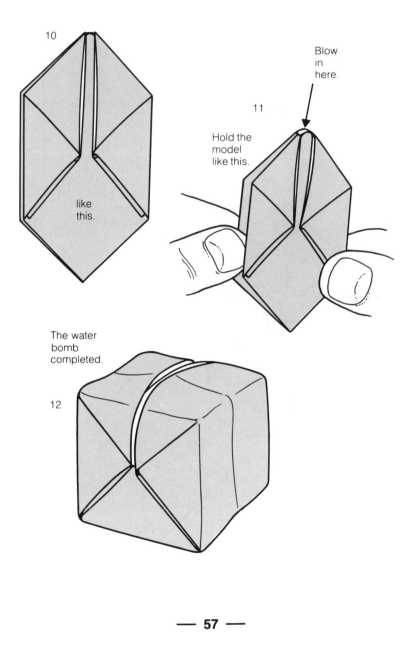

10

like
this.

Blow
in
here.

11

Hold the
model
like this.

The water
bomb
completed.

12

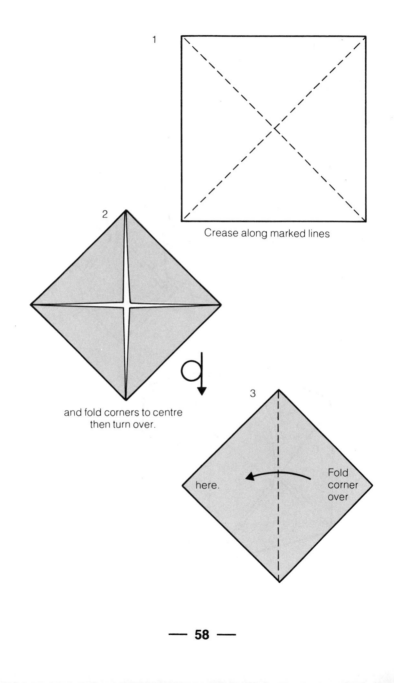

1

Crease along marked lines

2

and fold corners to centre
then turn over.

3

here.

Fold
corner
over

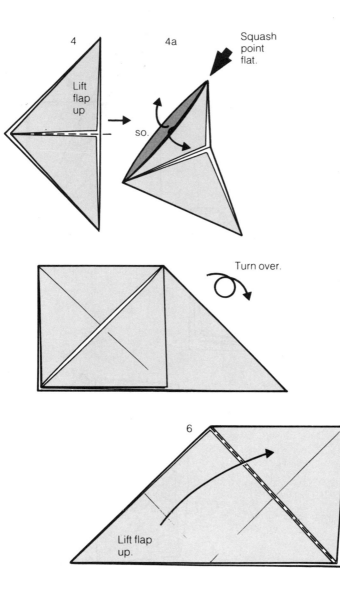

4

Lift
flap
up

4a

so.

Squash
point
flat.

Turn over.

6

Lift flap
up.

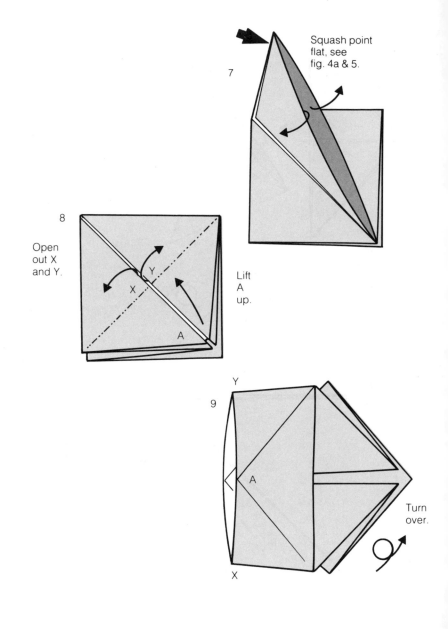

7

Squash point flat, see fig. 4a & 5.

8

Open out X and Y.

Y

X

A

Lift A up.

9

Y

A

X

Turn over.

Open out X and Y.

Lift A
up
as in
fig. 8
and
9

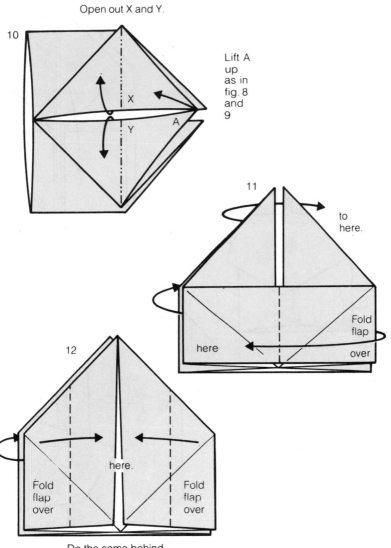

to
here.

Fold
flap
over

here

here.

Fold
flap
over

Fold
flap
over

Do the same behind.

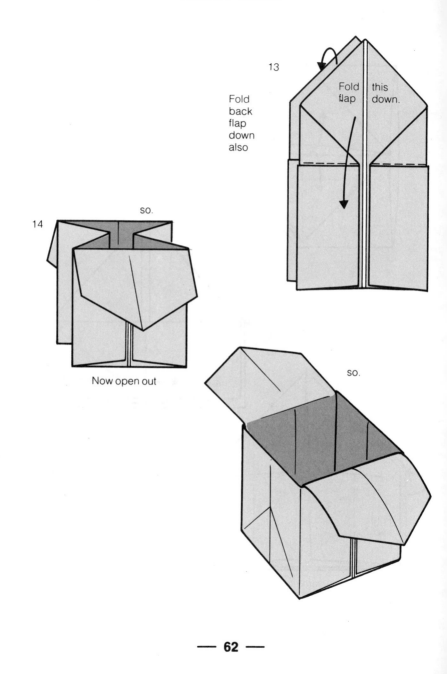

13

Fold flap | this down.

Fold back flap down also

so.

14

Now open out

so.

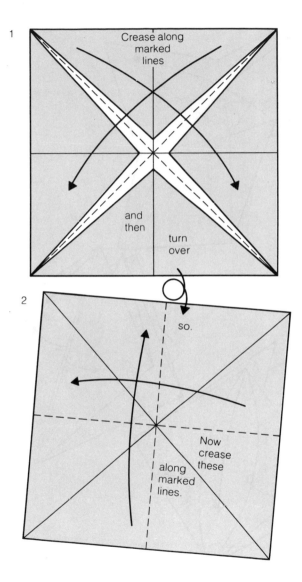

1 Crease along marked lines

and then

turn over

2 so.

Now crease these along marked lines.

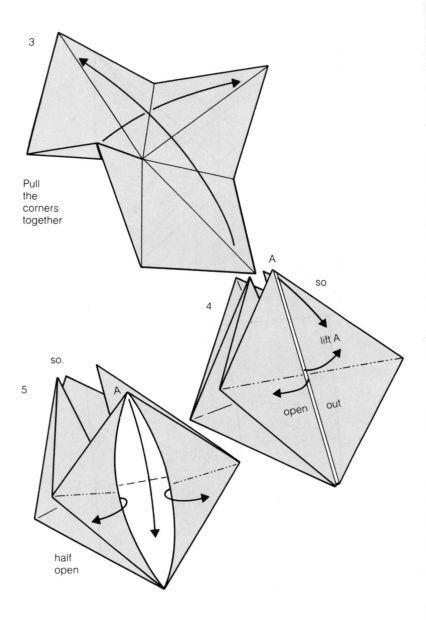

3

Pull
the
corners
together

A

so

4

lift A

open    out

so.

5

A

half
open

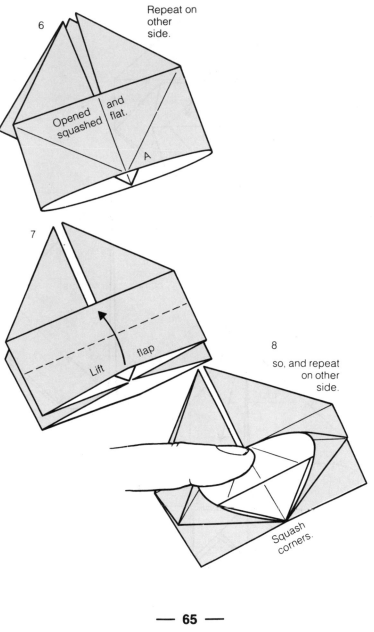

6

Repeat on
other
side.

Opened
squashed | and
flat.

A

7

Lift    flap

8

so, and repeat
on other
side.

Squash
corners.

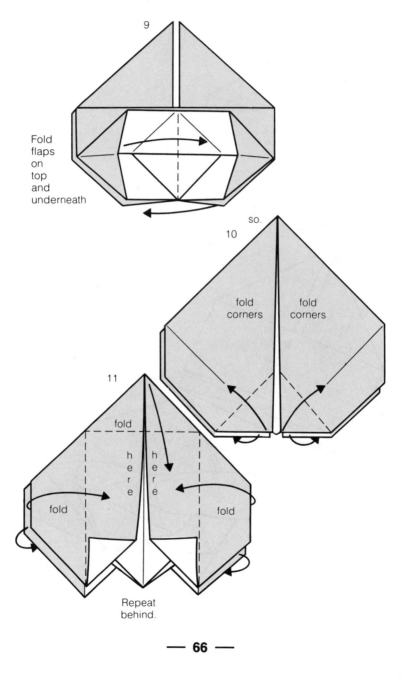

9

Fold
flaps
on
top
and
underneath

so.

10

fold
corners

fold
corners

11

fold

h
e
r
e

h
e
r
e

fold

fold

Repeat
behind.

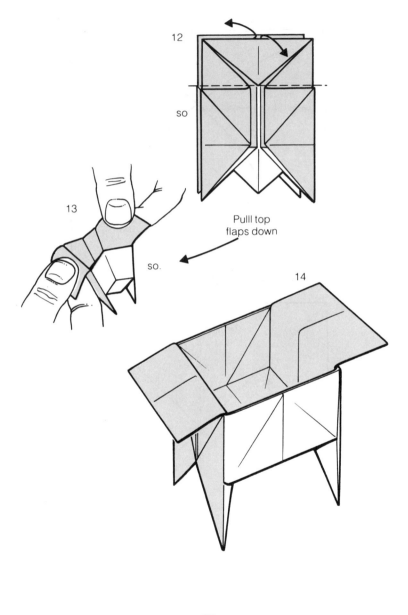

12

so

13

Pulll top
flaps down

so.

14

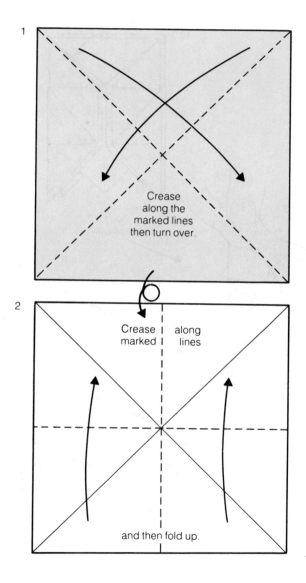

1

Crease
along the
marked lines
then turn over.

2

Crease | along
marked | lines

and then fold up.

3

so

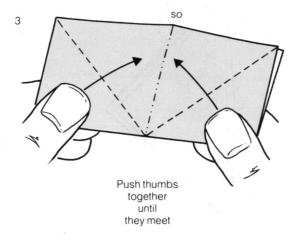

Push thumbs
together
until
they meet

so.

4

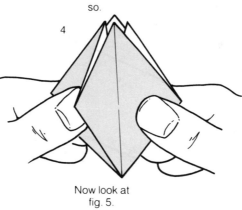

Now look at
fig. 5.

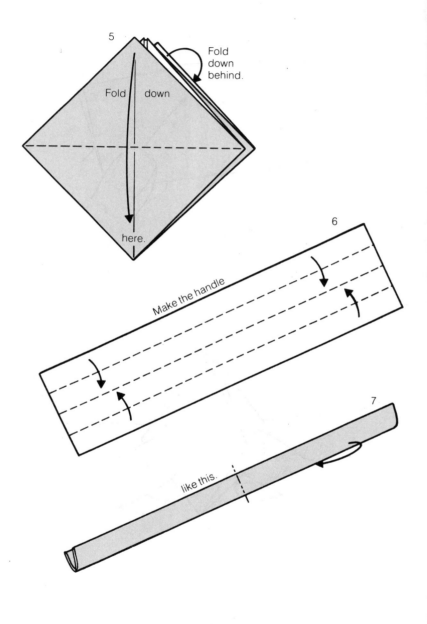

5

Fold down behind.

Fold down

here.

6

Make the handle

7

like this.

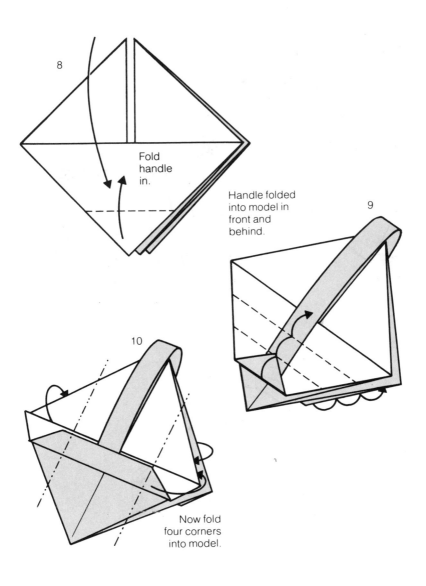

8

Fold
handle
in.

Handle folded
into model in
front and
behind.

9

10

Now fold
four corners
into model.

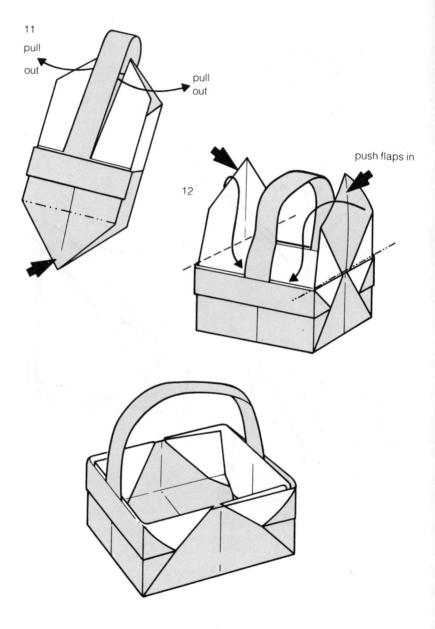

11
pull
out

pull
out

12

push flaps in

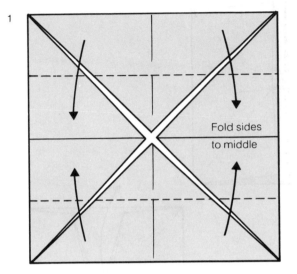

1

Fold sides
to middle

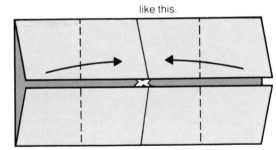

like this.

2

Fold sides to the middle.

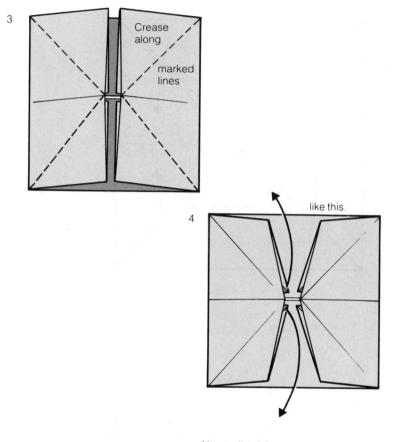

3

Crease
along

marked
lines

4

like this.

Now pull out the
two arrowed
points. The creases
will guide you and
they will fall into
place as in fig. 5

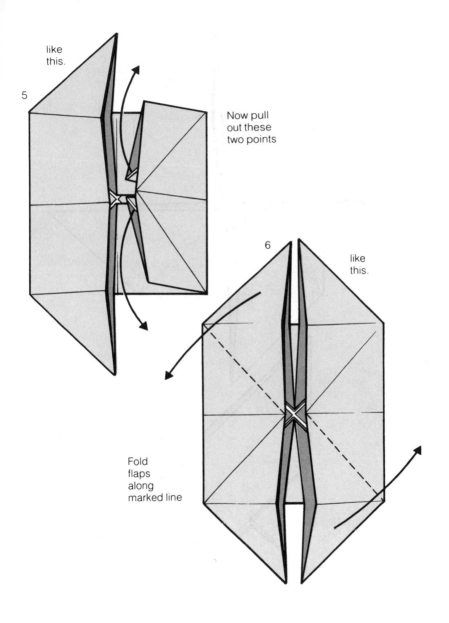

like
this.

5

Now pull
out these
two points

6

like
this.

Fold
flaps
along
marked line

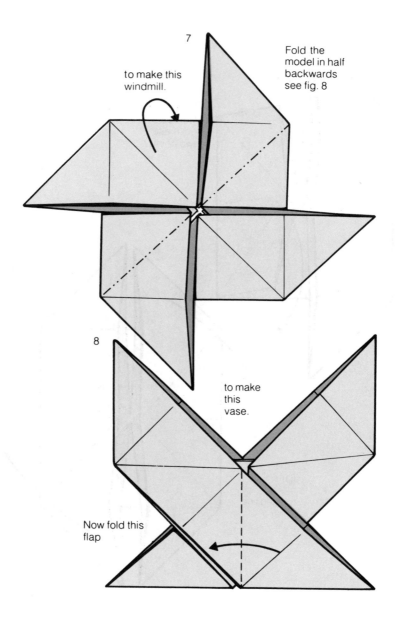

7

to make this
windmill.

Fold the
model in half
backwards
see fig. 8

8

to make
this
vase.

Now fold this
flap

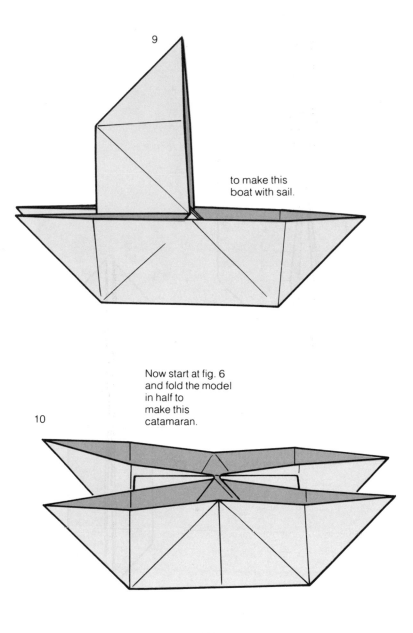

9

to make this
boat with sail.

Now start at fig. 6
and fold the model
in half to
make this
catamaran.

10

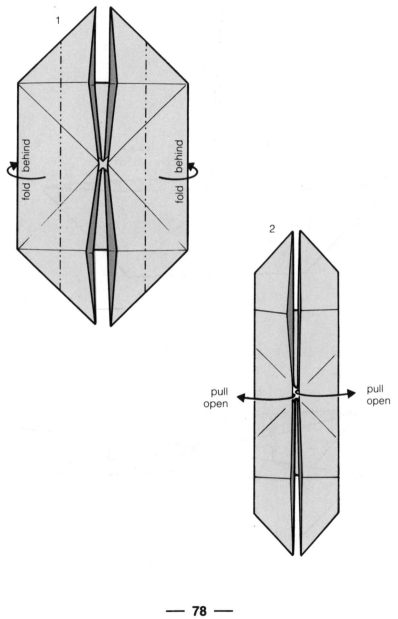

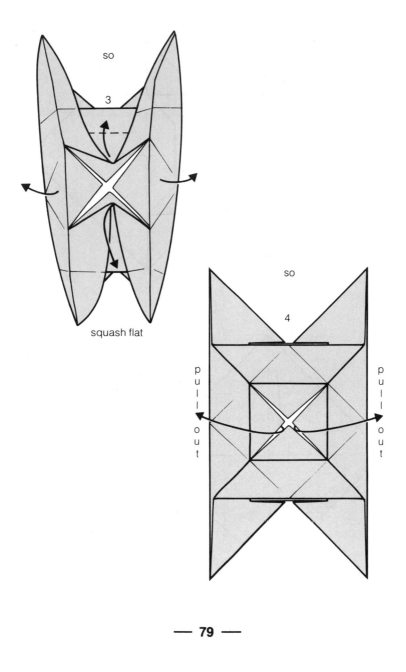

so

3

squash flat

so

4

p
u
l
l

o
u
t

p
u
l
l

o
u
t

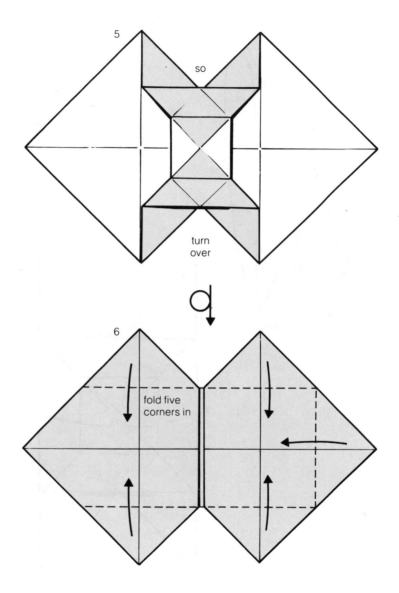

5

so

turn
over

6

fold five
corners in

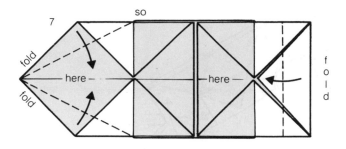

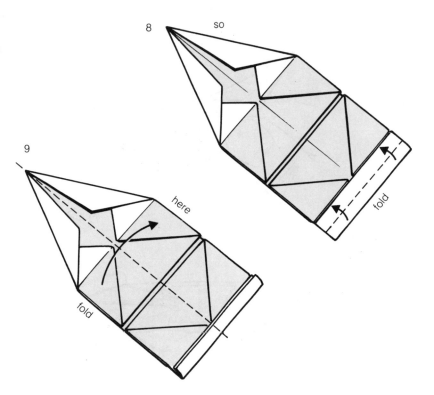

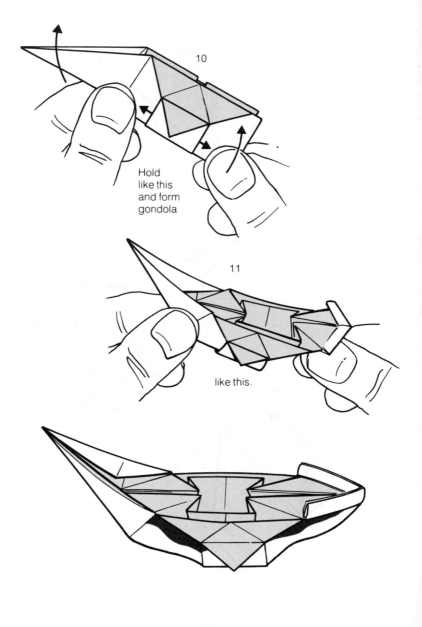

10

Hold
like this
and form
gondola

11

like this.

1
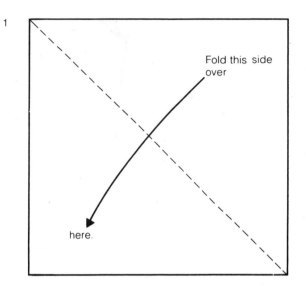

Fold this side over

here.

2
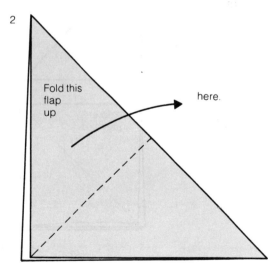

Fold this flap up

here.

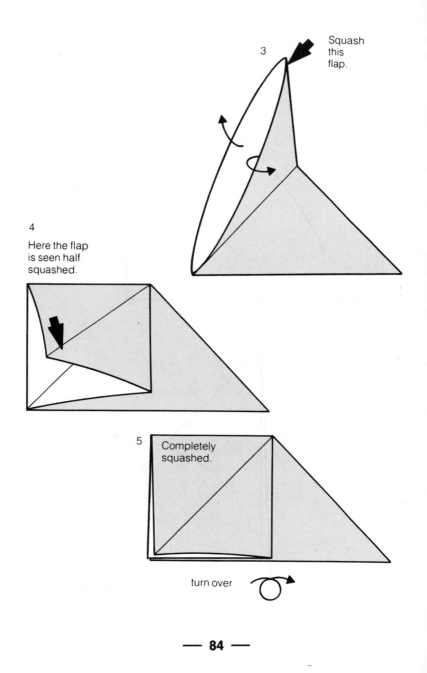

3

Squash
this
flap.

4

Here the flap
is seen half
squashed.

5

Completely
squashed.

turn over

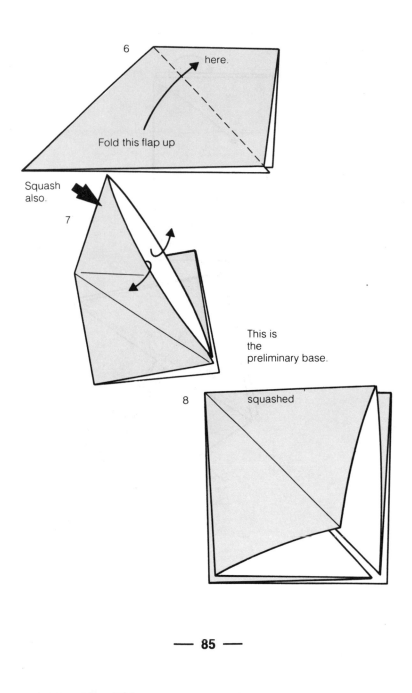

6

here.

Fold this flap up

Squash
also.

7

This is
the
preliminary base.

8 squashed

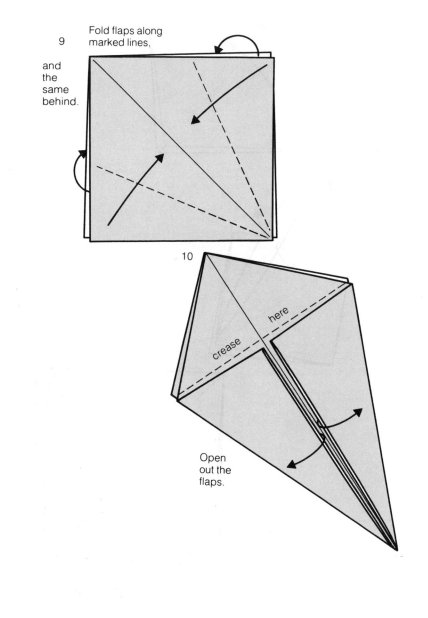

9 Fold flaps along marked lines,

and the same behind.

10 crease here

Open out the flaps.

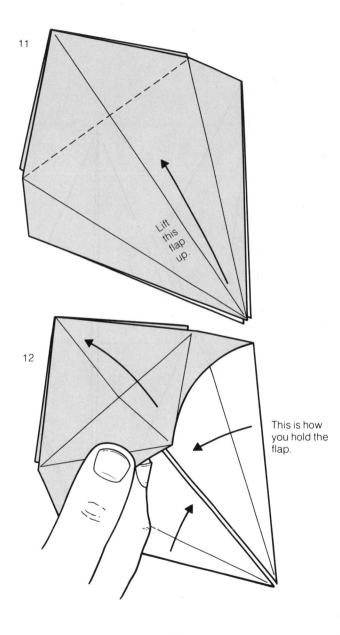

11

Lift
this
flap
up.

12

This is how
you hold the
flap.

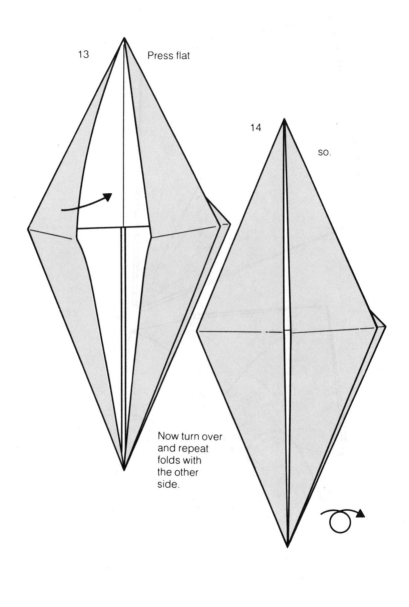

13  Press flat

Now turn over
and repeat
folds with
the other
side.

14

so.

15

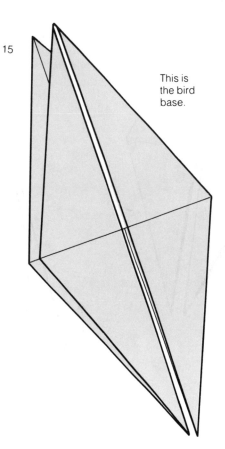

This is
the bird
base.

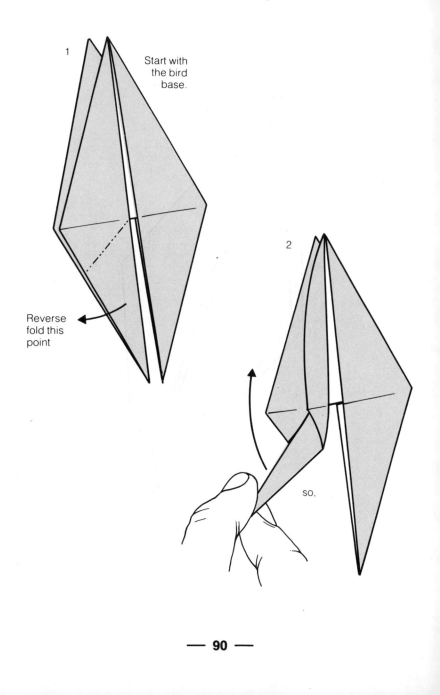

1

Start with
the bird
base.

Reverse
fold this
point

2

so,

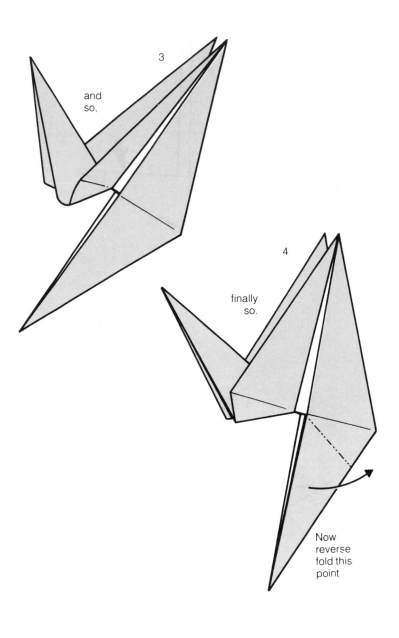

3

and
so,

4

finally
so.

Now
reverse
fold this
point

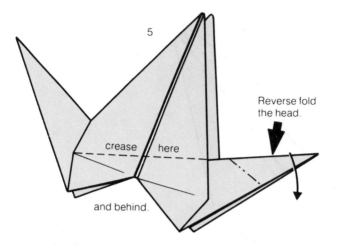

5

crease / here

and behind.

Reverse fold
the head.

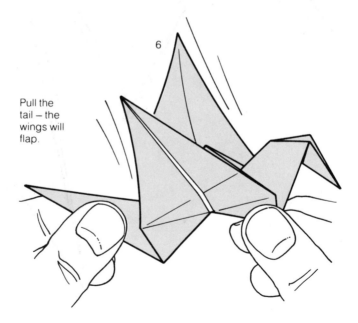

6

Pull the
tail – the
wings will
flap.

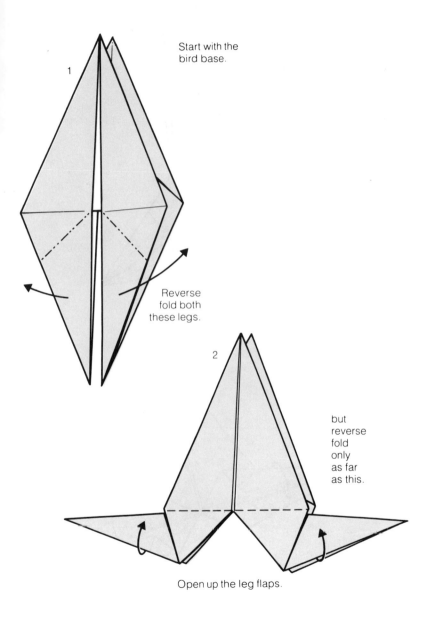

Start with the
bird base.

Reverse
fold both
these legs.

but
reverse
fold
only
as far
as this.

Open up the leg flaps.

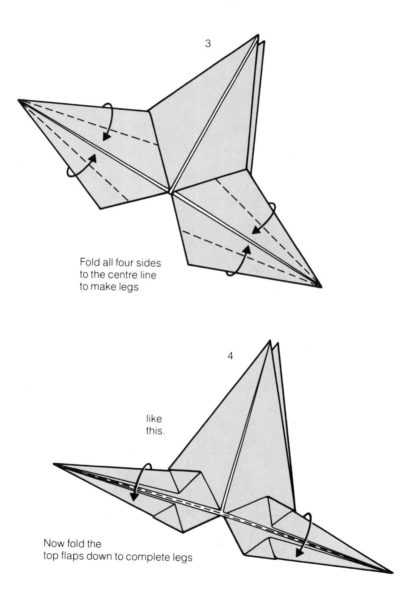

3

Fold all four sides
to the centre line
to make legs

4

like
this.

Now fold the
top flaps down to complete legs

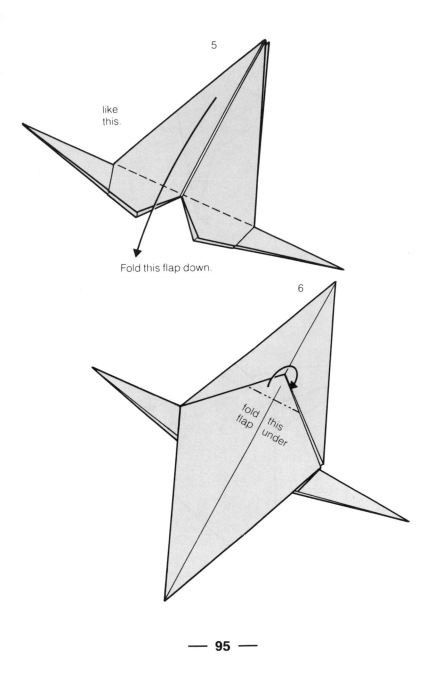

5

like
this.

Fold this flap down.

6

fold
flap this
under

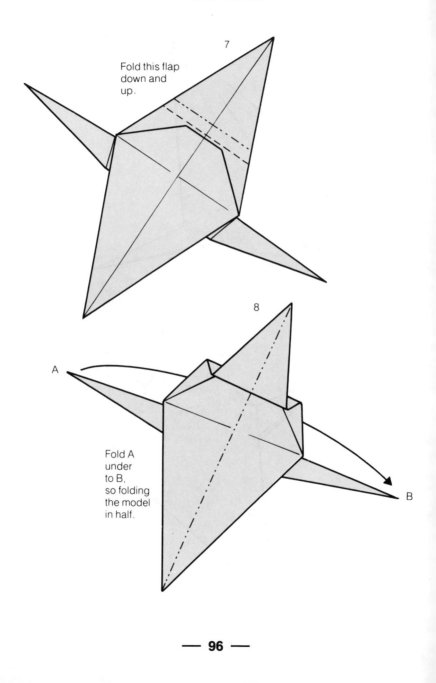

7

Fold this flap down and up.

8

A

Fold A under to B, so folding the model in half.

B

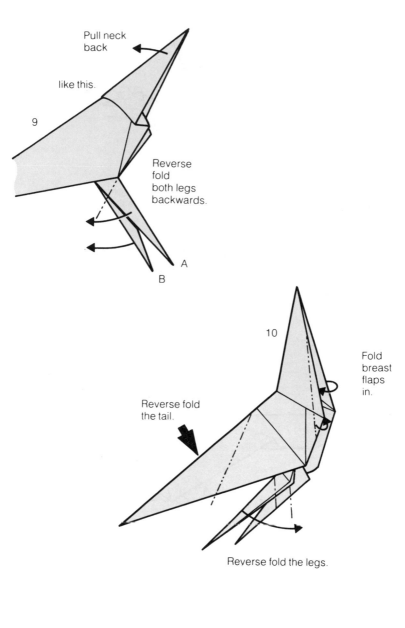

Pull neck back

like this.

9

Reverse fold both legs backwards.

A

B

10

Fold breast flaps in.

Reverse fold the tail.

Reverse fold the legs.

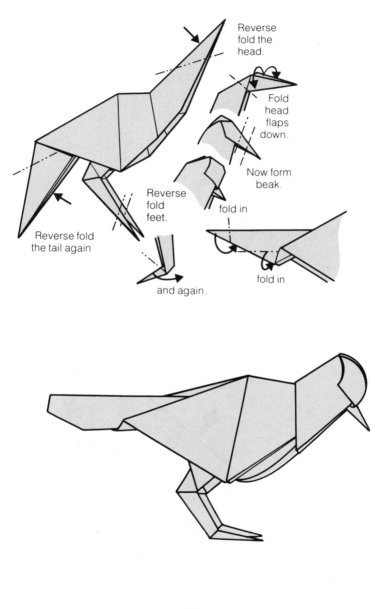

Reverse fold the head.

Fold head flaps down.

Now form beak.

fold in

fold in

Reverse fold feet.

Reverse fold the tail again

and again.

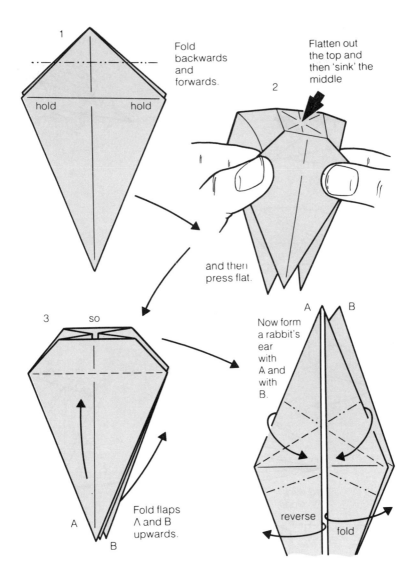

1

Fold
backwards
and
forwards.

hold          hold

Flatten out
the top and
then 'sink' the
middle

2

and then
press flat.

3      so

Now form
a rabbit's
ear
with
A and
with
B.

A      B

Fold flaps
∧ and B
upwards.

A

B

reverse      fold

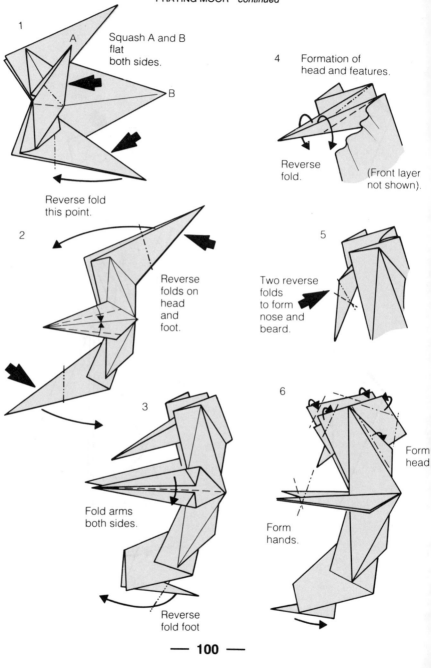

1

A

Squash A and B
flat
both sides.

B

Reverse fold
this point.

2

Reverse
folds on
head
and
foot.

3

Fold arms
both sides.

Reverse
fold foot

4    Formation of
head and features.

Reverse
fold.          (Front layer
              not shown).

5

Two reverse
folds
to form
nose and
beard.

6

Form
head

Form
hands.

The praying moor completed

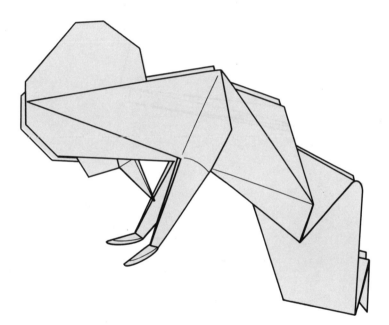

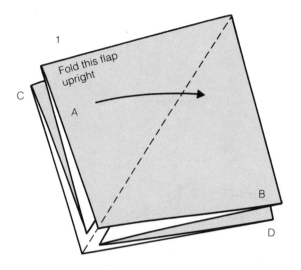

Fold this flap
upright

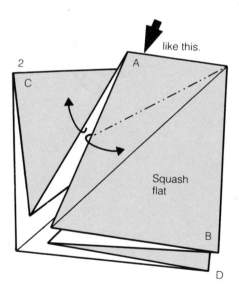

like this.

Squash
flat

3

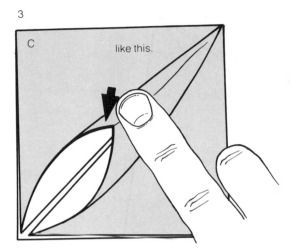

C

like this.

4

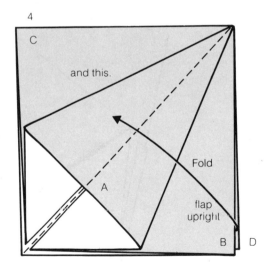

C

and this.

A

Fold

flap
upright

B    D

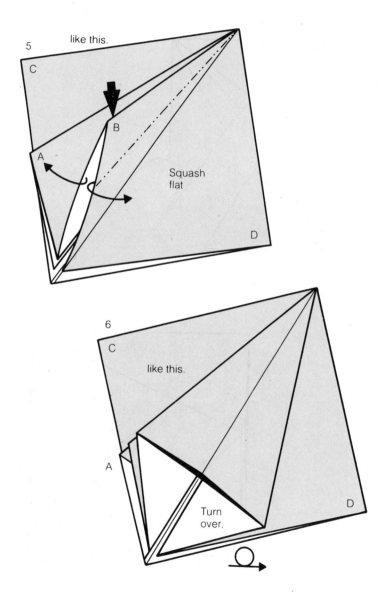

5  like this.

C

B

A

Squash flat

D

6  like this.

C

A

Turn over.

D

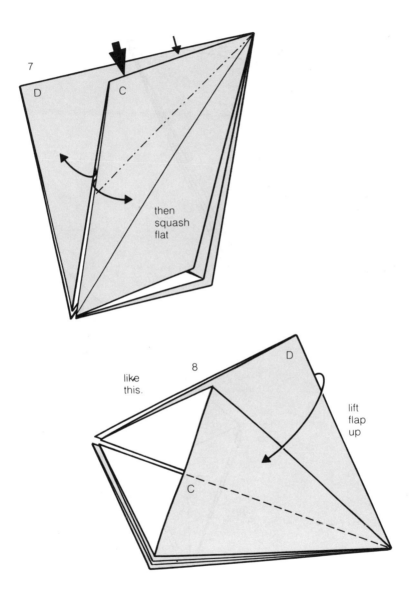

7

D

C

then
squash
flat

like
this.

8

D

lift
flap
up

C

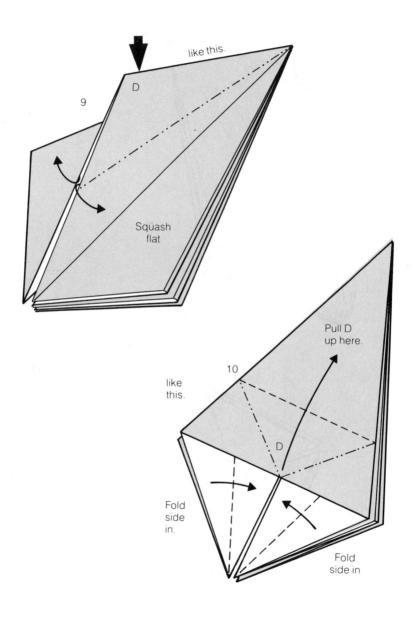

like this.

D

9

Squash
flat

Pull D
up here.

10

like
this.

D

Fold
side
in.

Fold
side in

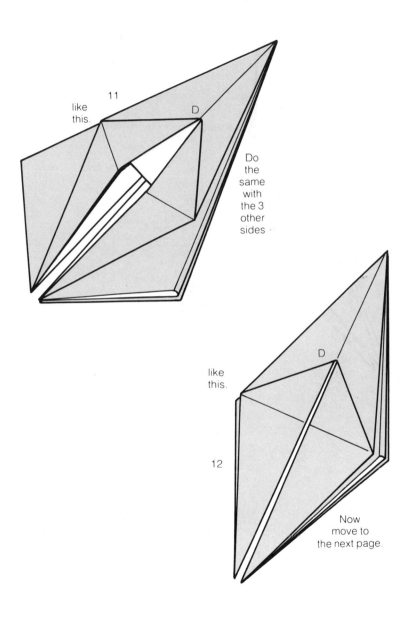

11

like
this.

D

Do
the
same
with
the 3
other
sides

like
this.

D

12

Now
move to
the next page.

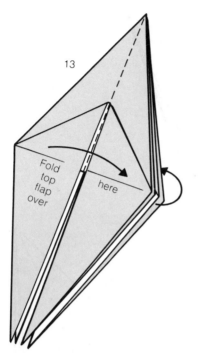

13

Fold
top
flap
over

here

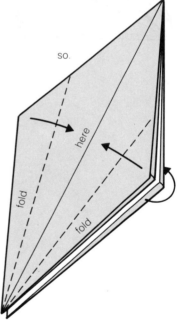

so.

here

fold

fold

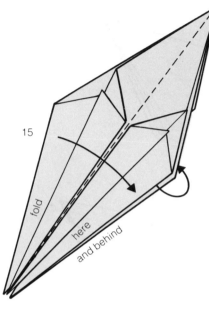

15 fold here and behind

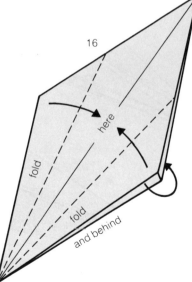

16 fold here fold and behind

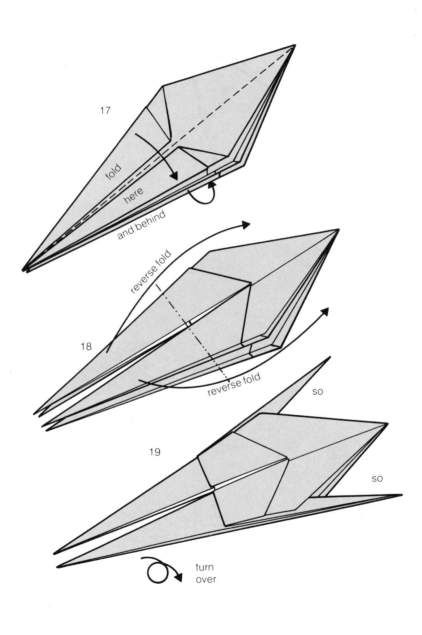

17

fold

here

and behind

18

reverse fold

reverse fold

19

so

so

turn
over

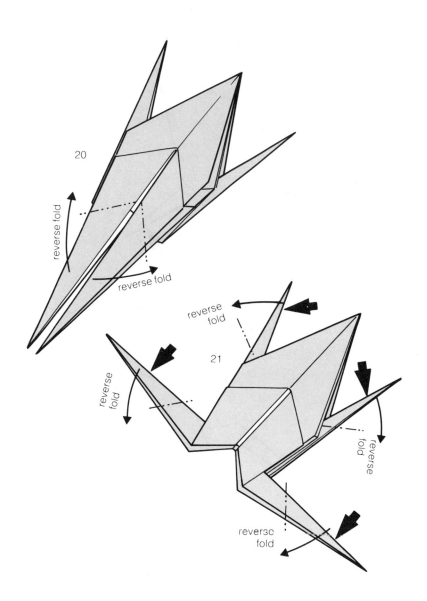

20

reverse fold

reverse fold

reverse fold

21

reverse fold

reverse fold

reverse fold

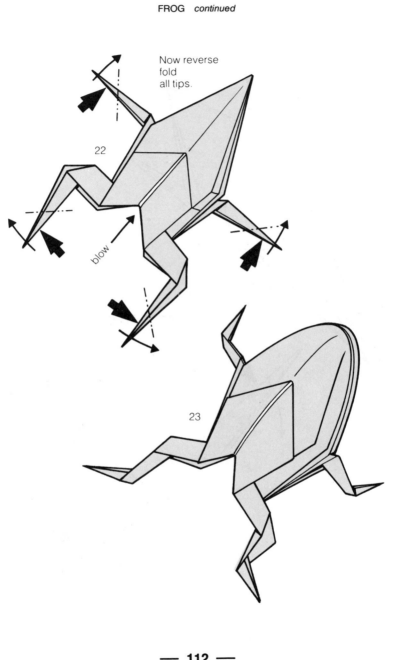

Now reverse
fold
all tips.

22

blow

23

## BAT MASK   *Peter Van Note, New York*

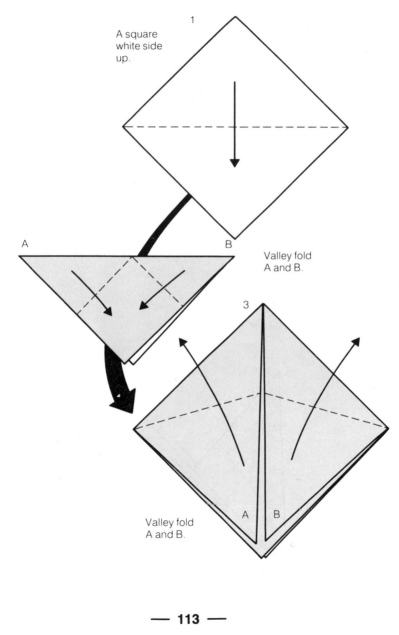

**1**

A square
white side
up.

**2**

A        B

Valley fold
A and B.

**3**

Valley fold
A and B.

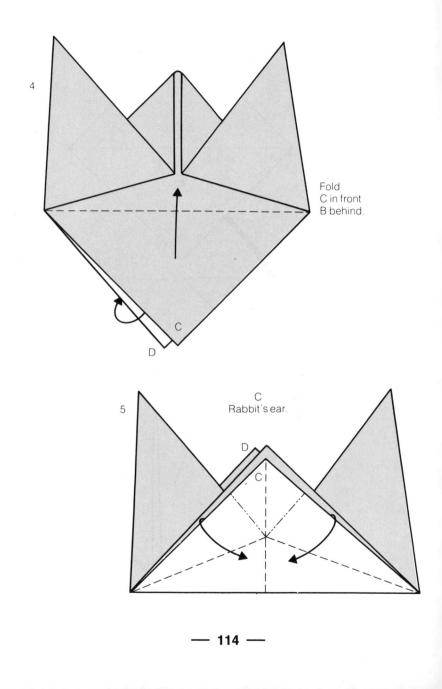

4

Fold
C in front
B behind.

C

D

5

C
Rabbit's ear.

D

C

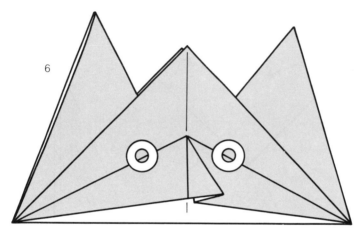

Make eyes with gummed eyelets.

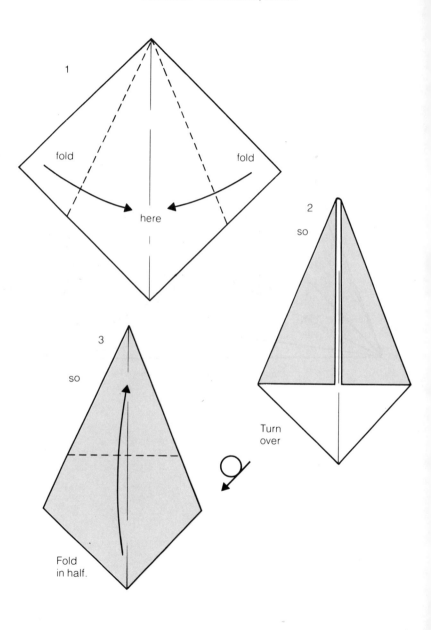

1

fold     fold

fold here

2

so

Turn over

3

so

Fold in half.

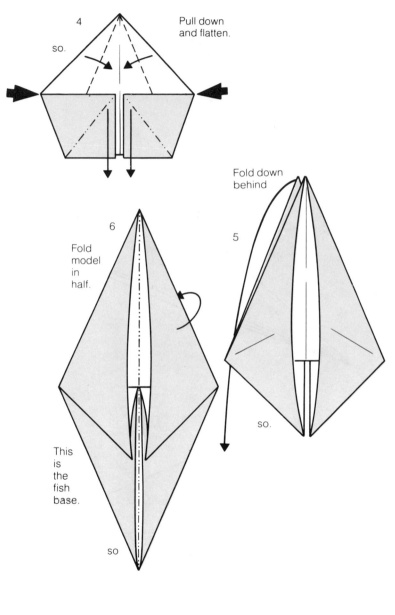

4

so.

Pull down
and flatten.

6

Fold
model
in
half.

This
is
the
fish
base.

so

Fold down
behind

5

so.

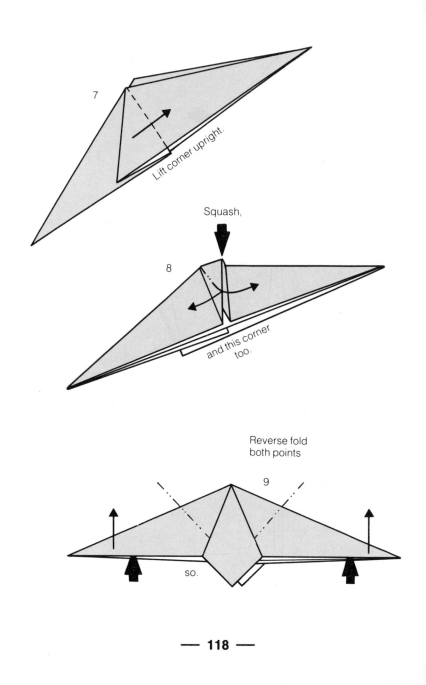

7

Lift corner upright.

Squash,

8

and this corner too.

Reverse fold both points

9

so.

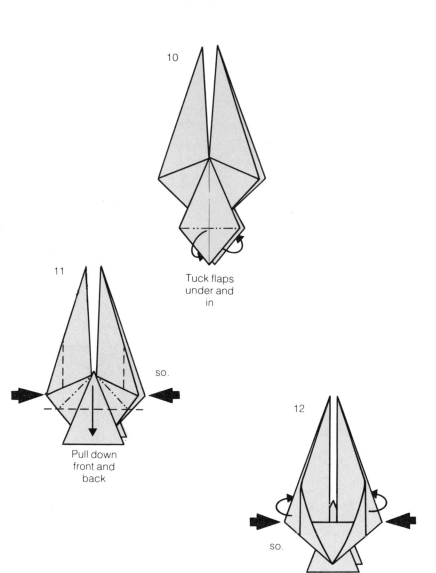

10

Tuck flaps
under and
in

11

so.

Pull down
front and
back

12

so.

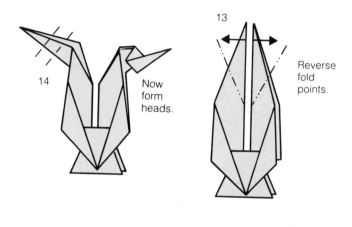

14

Now
form
heads.

13

Reverse
fold
points.

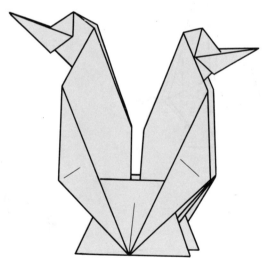

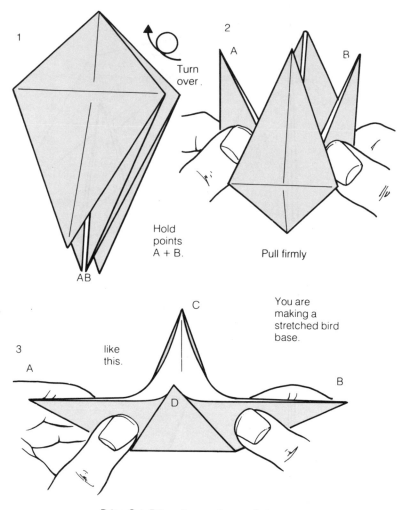

1   Turn over.

Hold points A + B.

AB

2   A   B

Pull firmly

You are making a stretched bird base.

3   like this.

A

C

D

B

Bring C + D together and press flat.

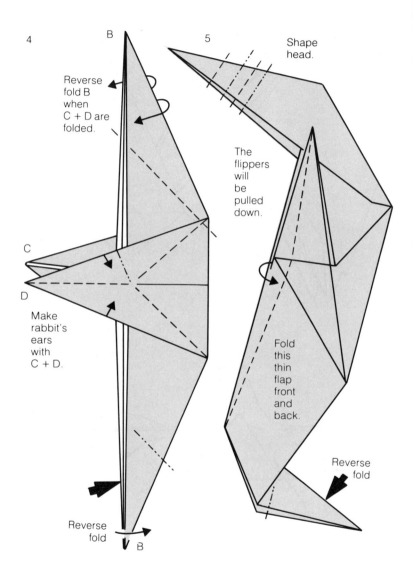

4

B

Reverse
fold B
when
C + D are
folded.

C

D

Make
rabbit's
ears
with
C + D.

Reverse
fold

B

5

Shape
head.

The
flippers
will
be
pulled
down.

Fold
this
thin
flap
front
and
back.

Reverse
fold

6

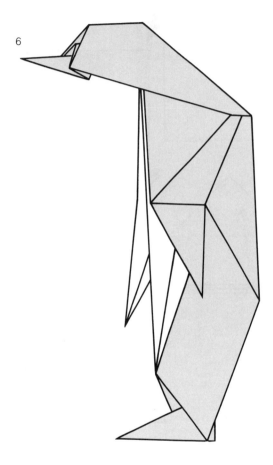

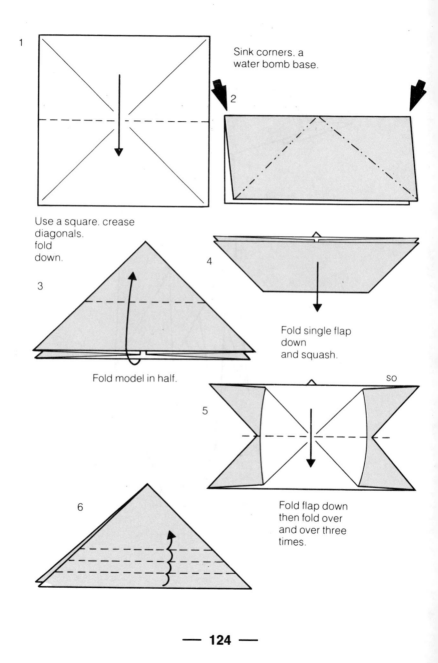

1

Sink corners. a
water bomb base.

2

Use a square. crease
diagonals.
fold
down.

3

4

Fold single flap
down
and squash.

Fold model in half.

5

so

6

Fold flap down
then fold over
and over three
times.

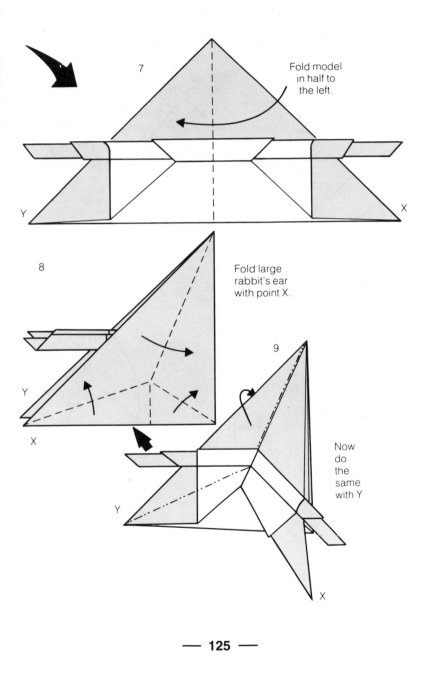

7

Fold model
in half to
the left.

Y

X

8

Fold large
rabbit's ear
with point X.

Y

X

9

Now
do
the
same
with Y

Y

X

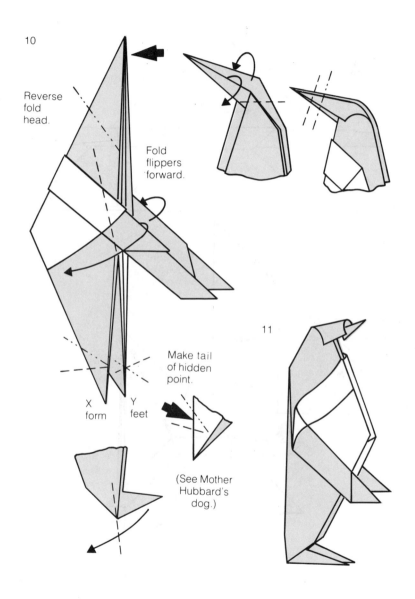

10

Reverse fold head.

Fold flippers forward.

X form

Y feet

Make tail of hidden point.

(See Mother Hubbard's dog.)

11

## RABBIT   *Michael P. Guy, Birmingham, England*

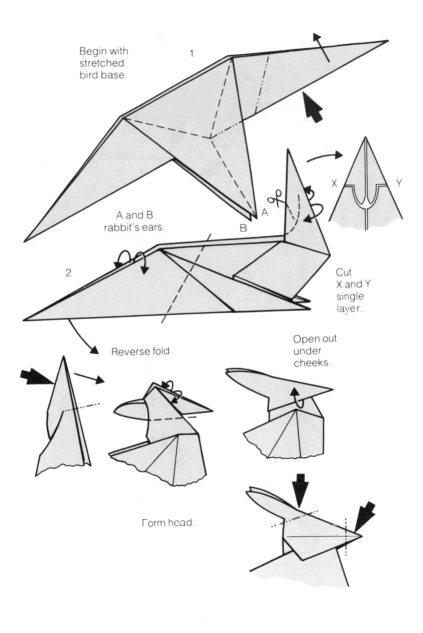

Begin with stretched bird base.

1

A and B rabbit's ears.

A

B

X     Y

Cut X and Y single layer.

2

Reverse fold.

Open out under cheeks.

Form head.

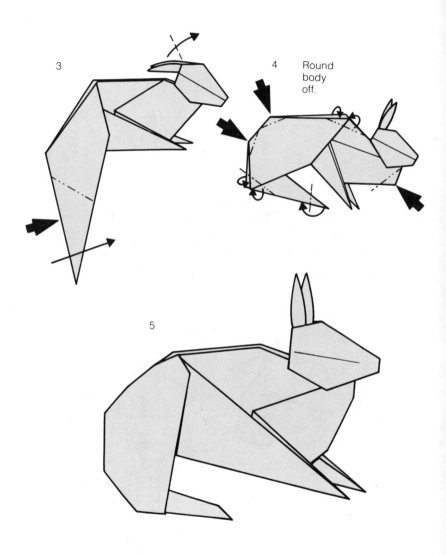

3

4 Round body off.

5

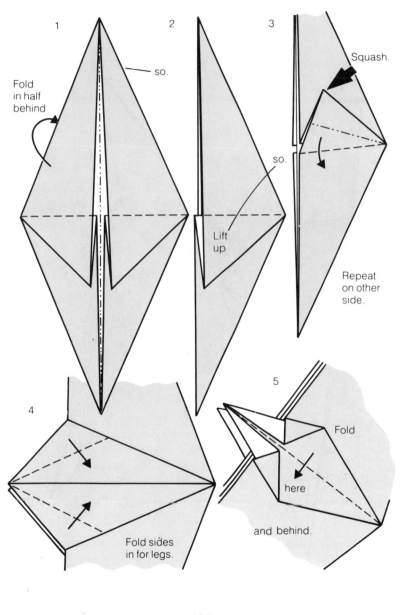

1

so.

Fold
in half
behind

2

so.

Lift
up

3

Squash.

Repeat
on other
side.

4

Fold sides
in for legs.

5

Fold

here

and behind.

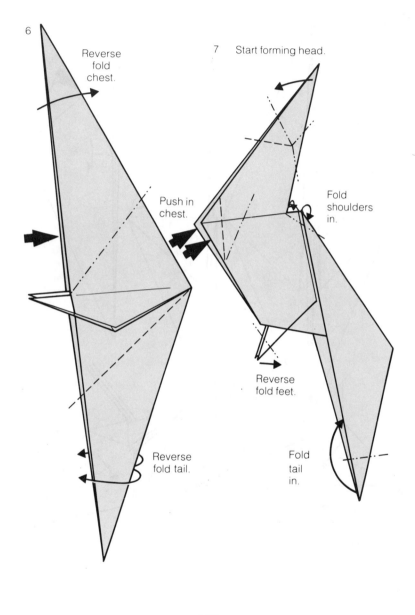

6

Reverse fold chest.

Push in chest.

Reverse fold tail.

7 Start forming head.

Fold shoulders in.

Reverse fold feet.

Fold tail in.

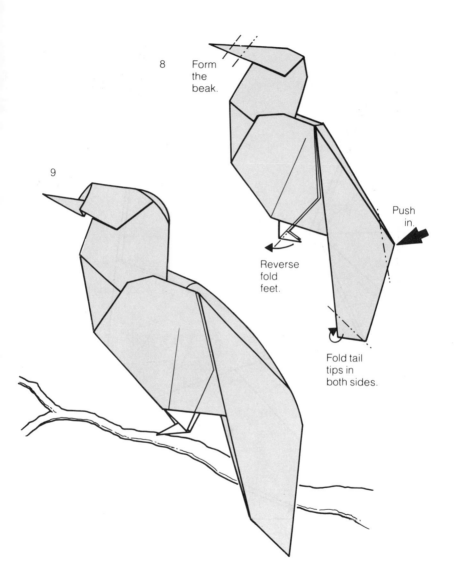

8 Form the beak.

9

Push in.

Reverse fold feet.

Fold tail tips in both sides.

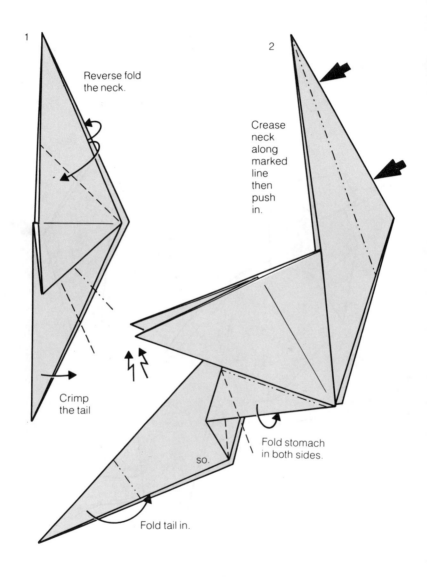

1

Reverse fold
the neck.

Crimp
the tail

2

Crease
neck
along
marked
line
then
push
in.

Fold stomach
in both sides.

so.

Fold tail in.

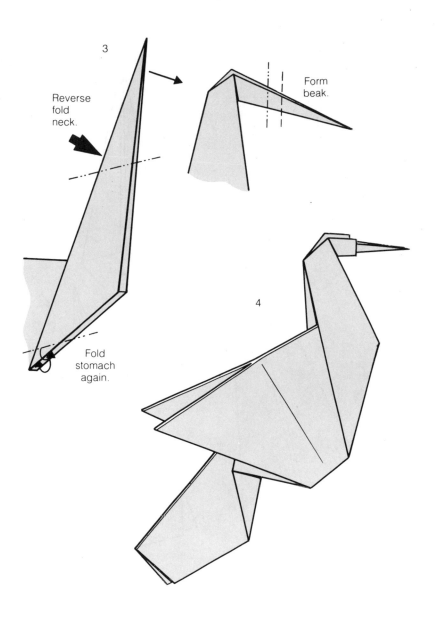

3

Reverse
fold
neck.

Form
beak.

Fold
stomach
again.

4

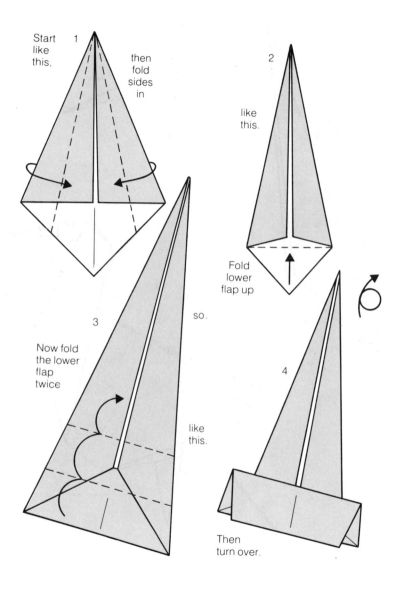

Start
like
this,

1

then
fold
sides
in

2

like
this.

Fold
lower
flap up

3

so.

Now fold
the lower
flap
twice

like
this.

4

Then
turn over.

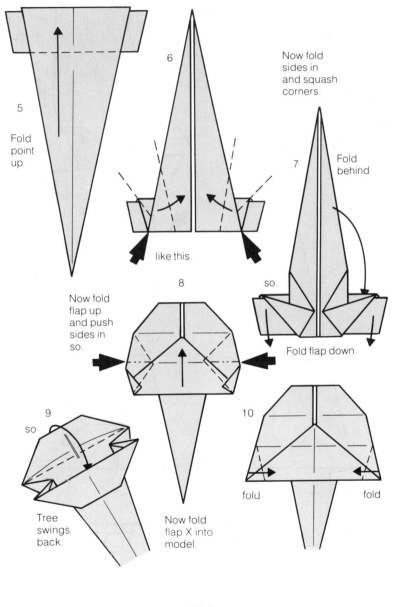

5

Fold point up

6

Now fold sides in and squash corners.

7

Fold behind

like this.

so.

Fold flap down.

8

Now fold flap up and push sides in so.

9

so

Tree swings back.

Now fold flap X into model.

10

fold

fold

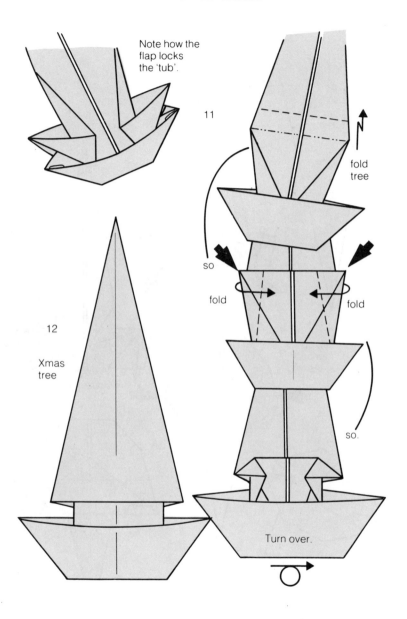

Note how the flap locks the 'tub'.

11

N

fold tree

so

fold

fold

so.

12

Xmas tree

Turn over.

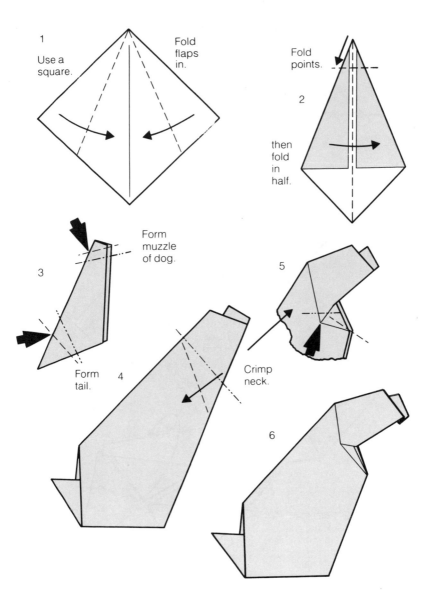

1
Use a square.
Fold flaps in.

Fold points.
2
then fold in half.

3
Form muzzle of dog.
Form tail.

5
Crimp neck.

4

6

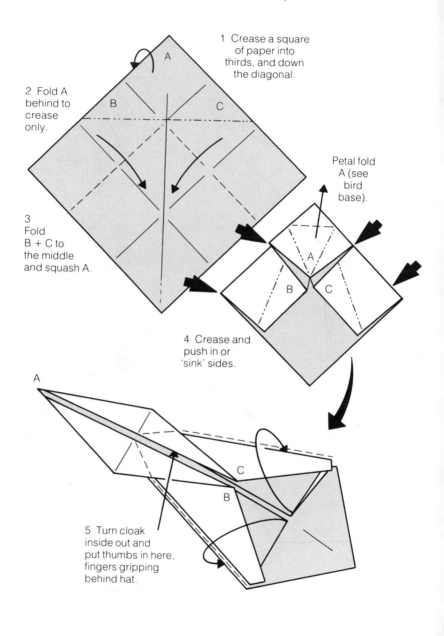

1 Crease a square
of paper into
thirds, and down
the diagonal.

2 Fold A
behind to
crease
only.

Petal fold
A (see
bird
base).

3
Fold
B + C to
the middle
and squash A.

4 Crease and
push in or
'sink' sides.

5 Turn cloak
inside out and
put thumbs in here,
fingers gripping
behind hat.

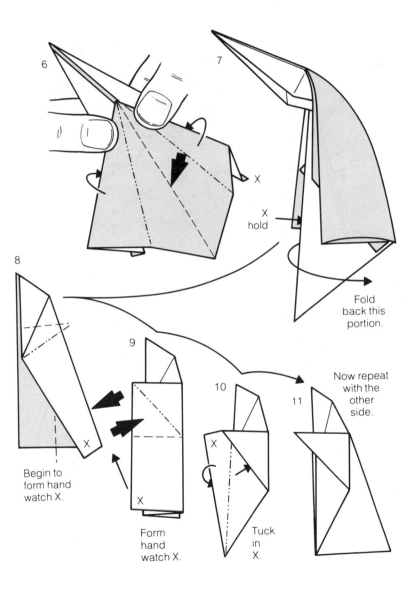

6

7

X

X
hold

Fold
back this
portion.

8

9

10

11

Now repeat
with the
other
side.

X

X

Begin to
form hand
watch X.

Form
hand
watch X.

X

X

Tuck
in
X.

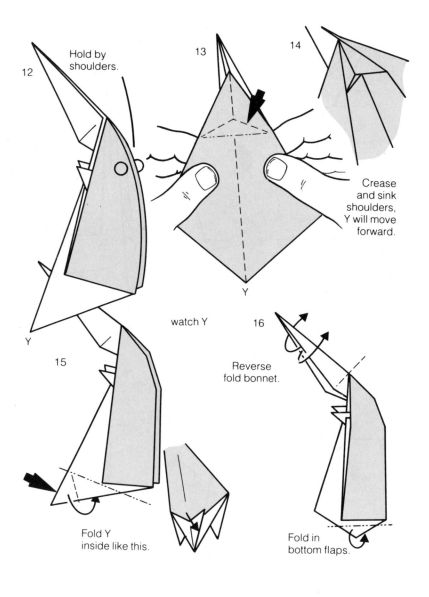

12

Hold by shoulders.

13

14

Crease and sink shoulders, Y will move forward.

Y

watch Y

15

Y

16

Reverse fold bonnet.

Fold Y inside like this.

Fold in bottom flaps.

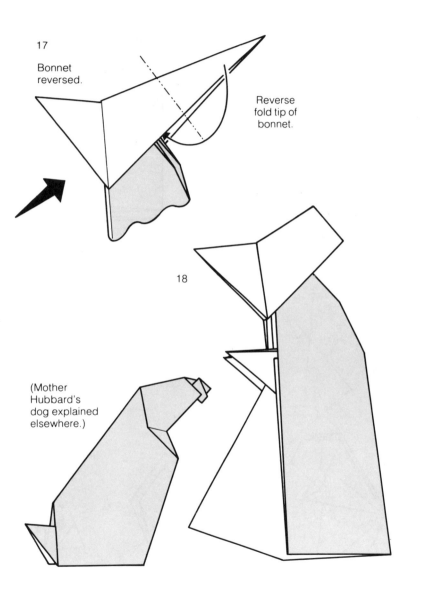

17

Bonnet
reversed.

Reverse
fold tip of
bonnet.

18

(Mother
Hubbard's
dog explained
elsewhere.)

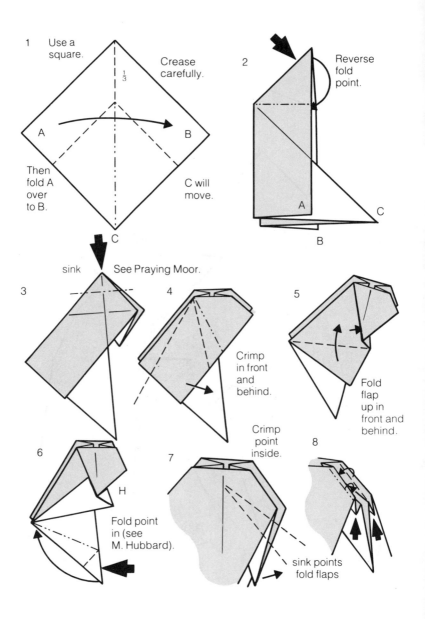

1  Use a square.

Crease carefully.

$\frac{1}{3}$

A

B

Then fold A over to B.

C will move.

C

2  Reverse fold point.

A

C

B

sink    See Praying Moor.

3

4  Crimp in front and behind.

5  Fold flap up in front and behind.

6  H  Fold point in (see M. Hubbard).

7  Crimp point inside.

8  sink points fold flaps

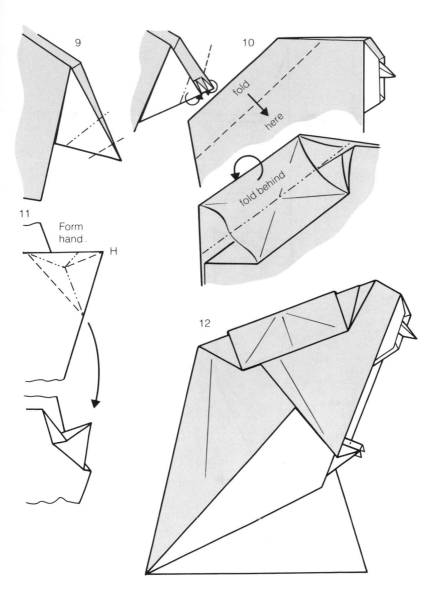

9

10

fold

here

fold behind

11

Form
hand.

H

12

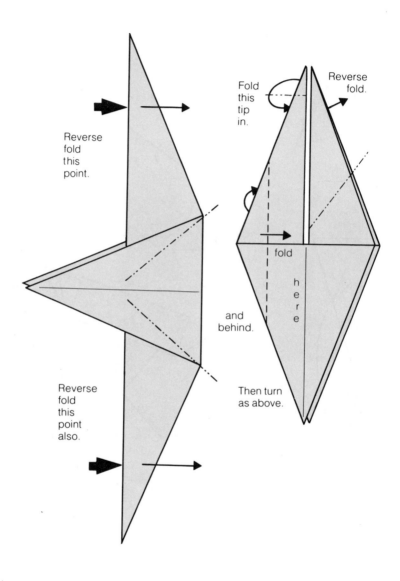

Reverse
fold
this
point.

Reverse
fold
this
point
also.

Fold
this
tip
in.

Reverse
fold.

fold

h
e
r
e

and
behind.

Then turn
as above.

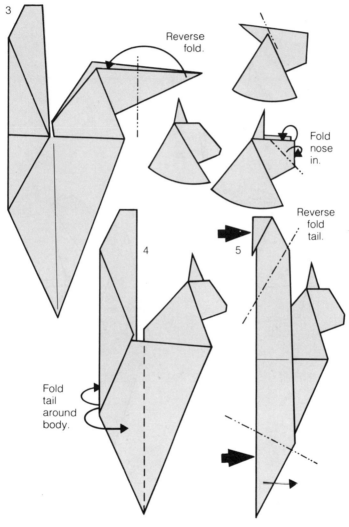

3

Reverse
fold.

Fold
nose
in.

Reverse
fold
tail.

4

5

Fold
tail
around
body.

Reverse fold legs.

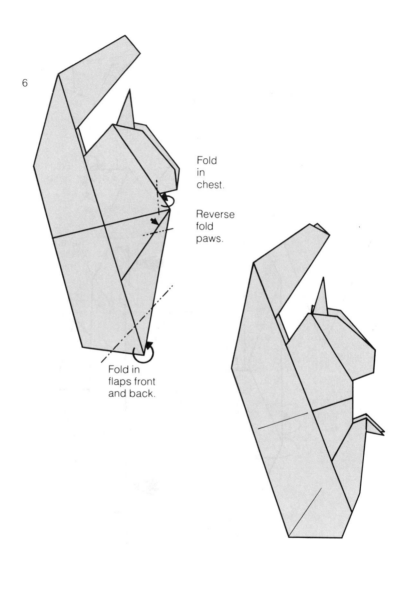

6

Fold
in
chest.

Reverse
fold
paws.

Fold in
flaps front
and back.

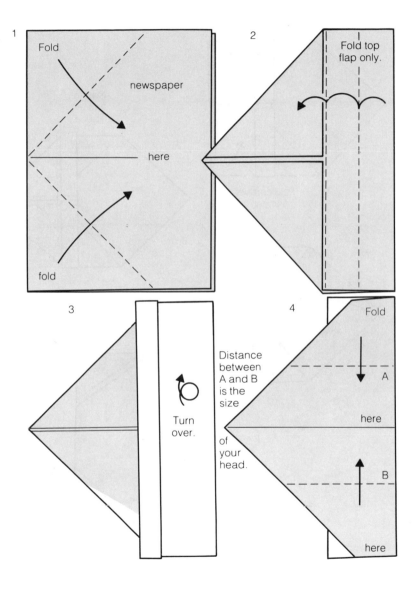

1

Fold

newspaper

here

fold

2

Fold top flap only.

3

Turn over.

Distance between A and B is the size of your head.

4

Fold

A

here

B

here

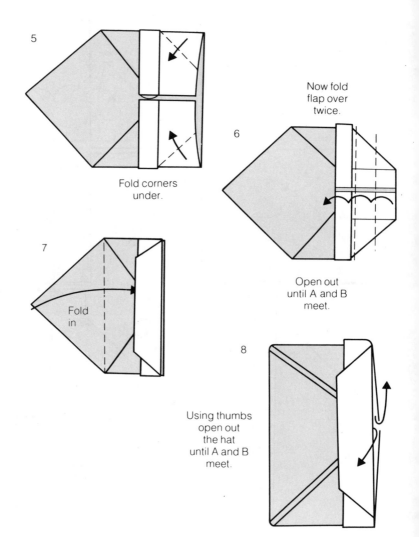

5

Fold corners under.

Now fold flap over twice.

6

Open out until A and B meet.

7

Fold in

8

Using thumbs open out the hat until A and B meet.

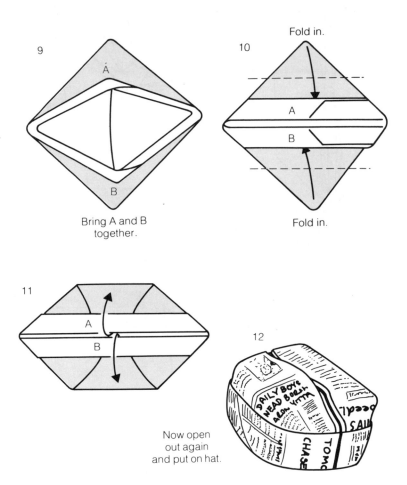

9

Bring A and B
together.

10

Fold in.

Fold in.

11

Now open
out again
and put on hat.

12

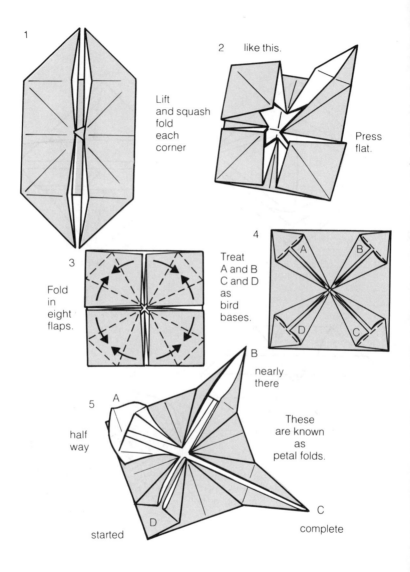

1

2   like this.

Lift
and squash
fold
each
corner

Press
flat.

3

Fold
in
eight
flaps.

4

Treat
A and B
C and D
as
bird
bases.

A   B

D   C

5

A

B

nearly
there

half
way

These
are known
as
petal folds.

started

D

C

complete

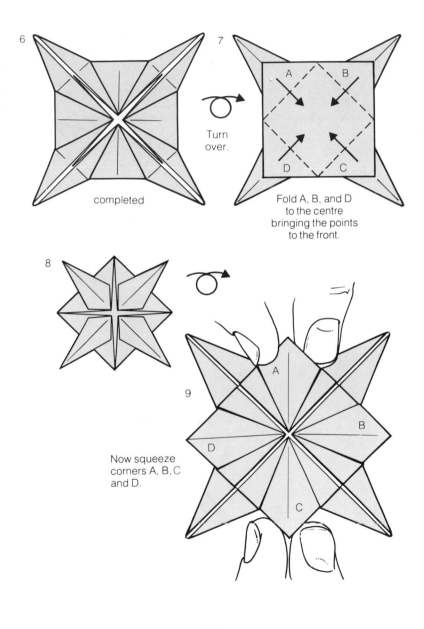

6

completed

Turn
over.

7

A          B

D          C

Fold A, B, and D
to the centre
bringing the points
to the front.

8

9

A

B

D

C

Now squeeze
corners A, B, C
and D.

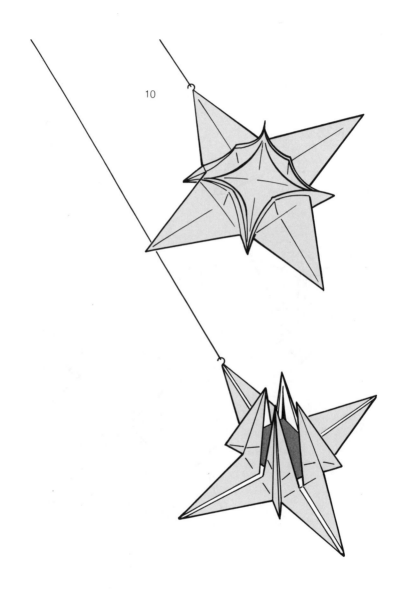

10

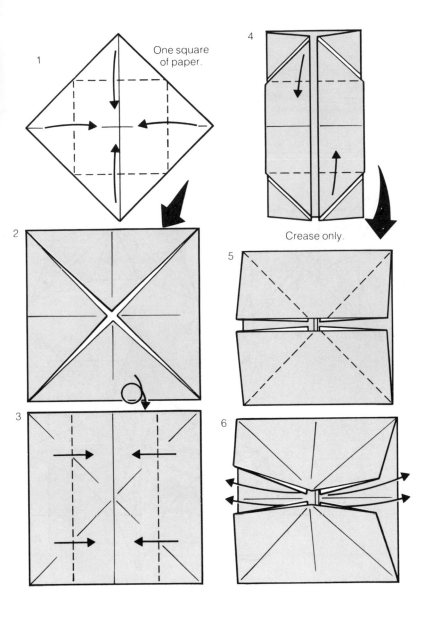

1 One square of paper.

4

Crease only.

2

3

5

6

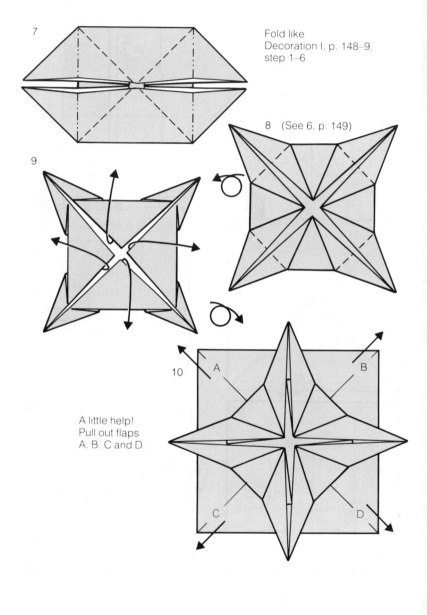

7

Fold like
Decoration I, p. 148–9,
step 1–6

8   (See 6, p. 149)

9

10

A little help!
Pull out flaps
A. B. C and D.

A

B

C

D

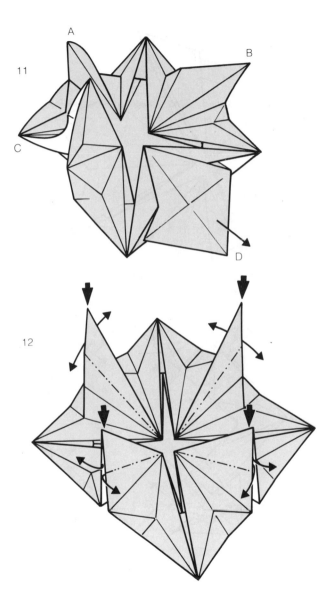

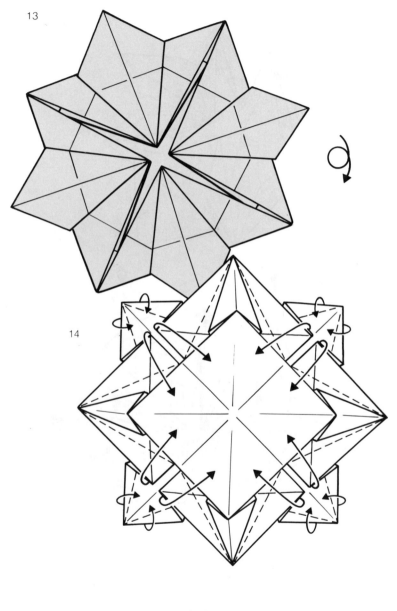

13

14

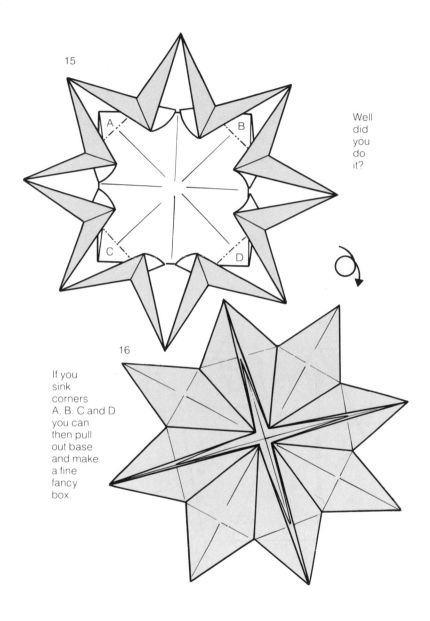

15

Well
did
you
do
it?

If you
sink
corners
A. B. C and D
you can
then pull
out base
and make
a fine
fancy
box.

16

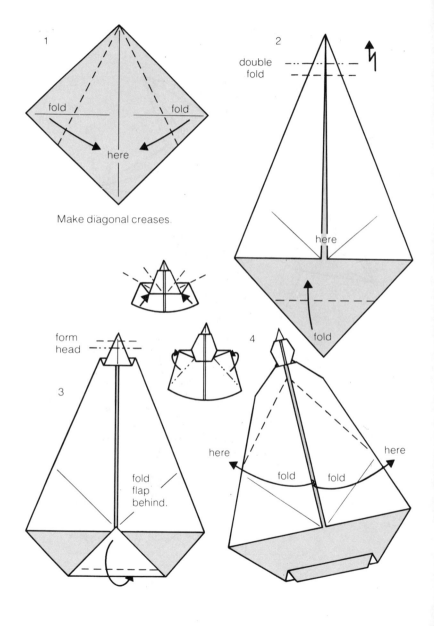

1

fold        fold

here

Make diagonal creases.

2

double
fold

here

fold

form
head

3

fold
flap
behind.

4

here                    here

fold    fold

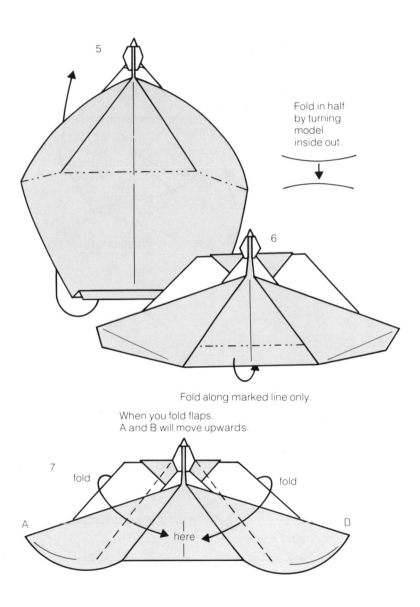

5

Fold in half
by turning
model
inside out.

6

Fold along marked line only.

When you fold flaps.
A and B will move upwards.

7

fold

fold

A

B

here

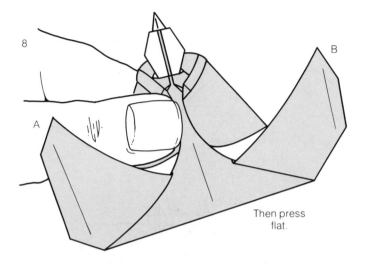

8

A

B

Then press
flat.

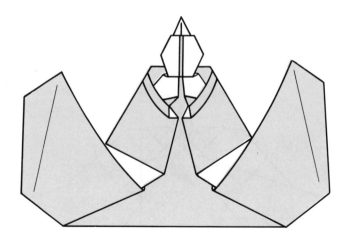

9

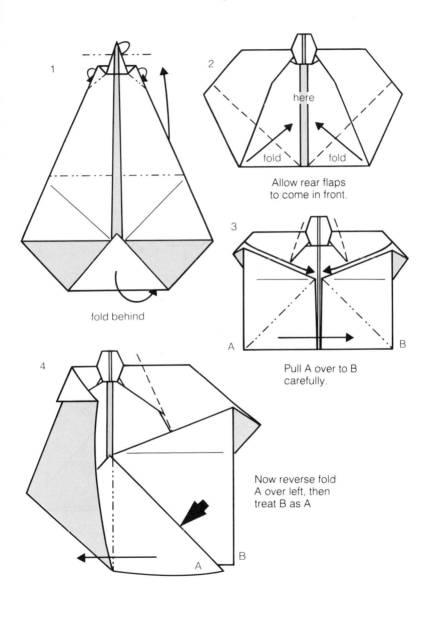

1

2

here

fold                    fold

Allow rear flaps
to come in front.

3

A                                    B

Pull A over to B
carefully.

fold behind

4

Now reverse fold
A over left, then
treat B as A

B

A

5

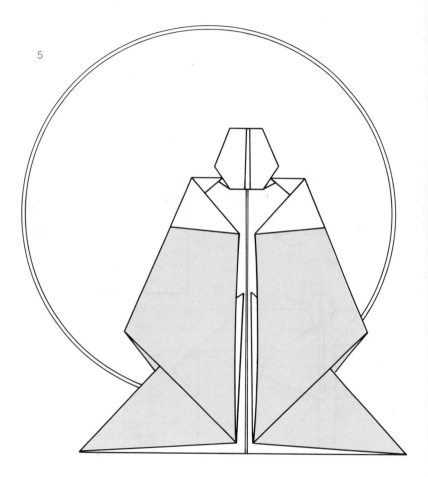

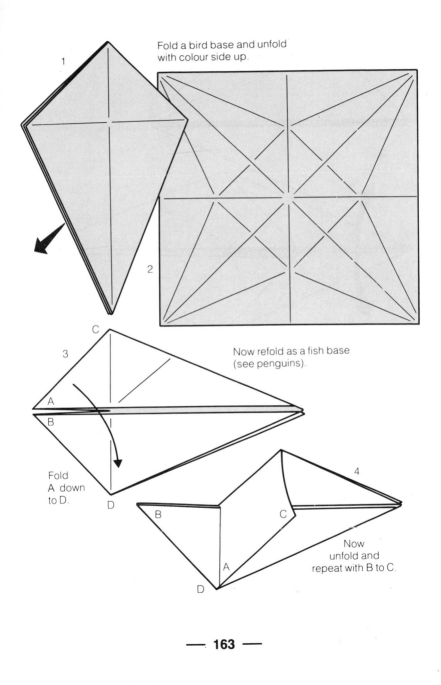

Fold a bird base and unfold with colour side up.

1

2

Now refold as a fish base (see penguins).

3

C

A

B

Fold
A down
to D.

D

4

B

C

A

D

Now
unfold and
repeat with B to C.

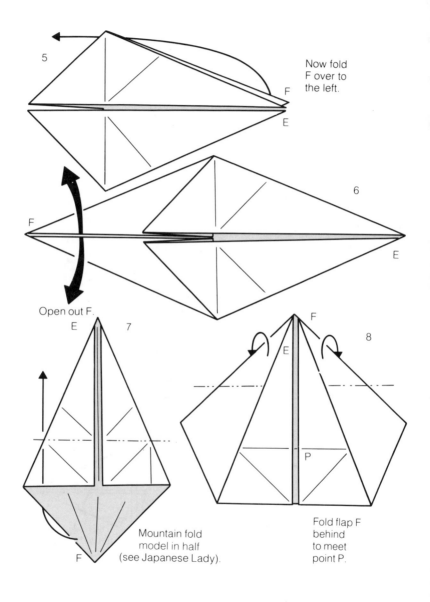

5

Now fold
F over to
the left.

F

E

6

F

E

Open out F.

E   7

Mountain fold
model in half
(see Japanese Lady).

F

F

8

E

P

Fold flap F
behind
to meet
point P.

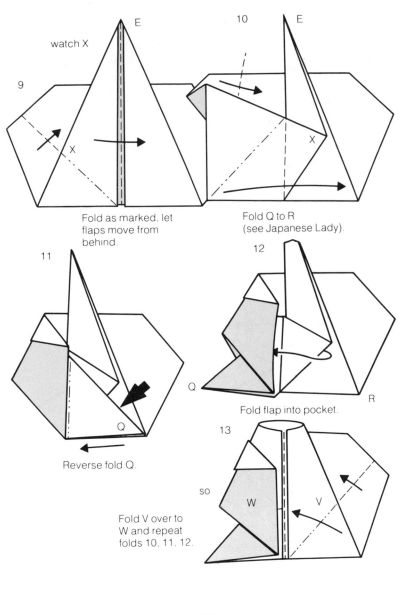

watch X

9

E

Fold as marked, let
flaps move from
behind.

10

E

X

Fold Q to R
(see Japanese Lady).

11

Q

Reverse fold Q.

12

Q

R

Fold flap into pocket.

13

so

W

V

Fold V over to
W and repeat
folds 10, 11, 12.

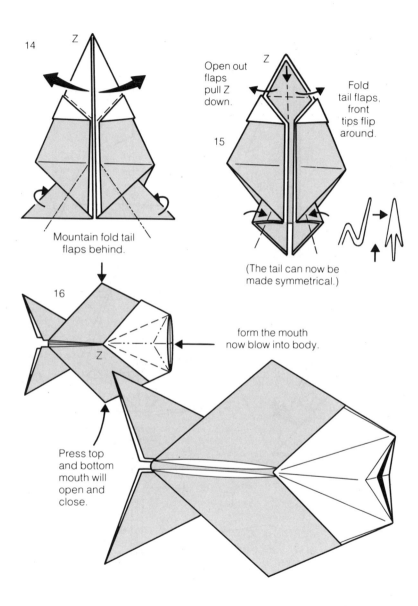

14

Z

Mountain fold tail flaps behind.

Open out flaps pull Z down.

Z

Fold tail flaps, front tips flip around.

15

(The tail can now be made symmetrical.)

16

Z

form the mouth now blow into body.

Press top and bottom mouth will open and close.

1  Start from white side of paper.

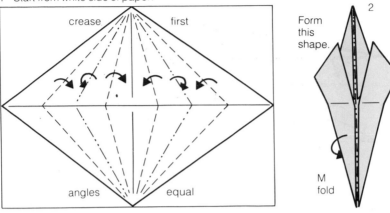

crease  first

Form
this
shape.

2

angles  equal

M
fold

Cut diamond from 4 × 3
rectangle.

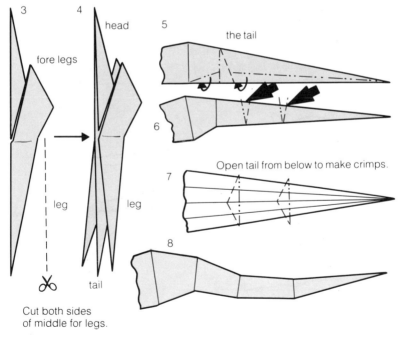

3  4

head

fore legs

5

the tail

6

leg  leg

Open tail from below to make crimps.

7

8

tail

Cut both sides
of middle for legs.

9    The head and neck.

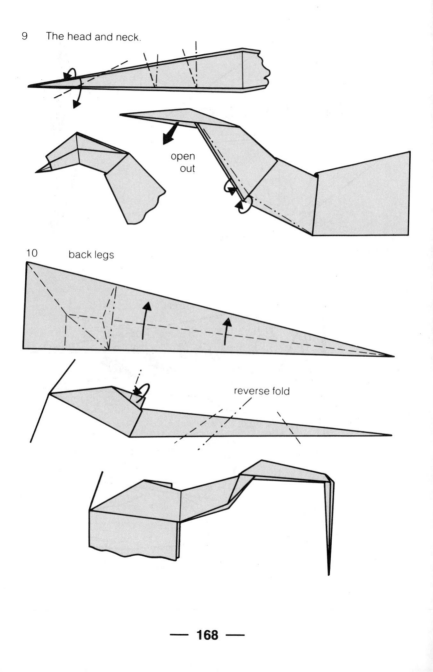

open
out

10    back legs

reverse fold

11 fore legs

12

13

14

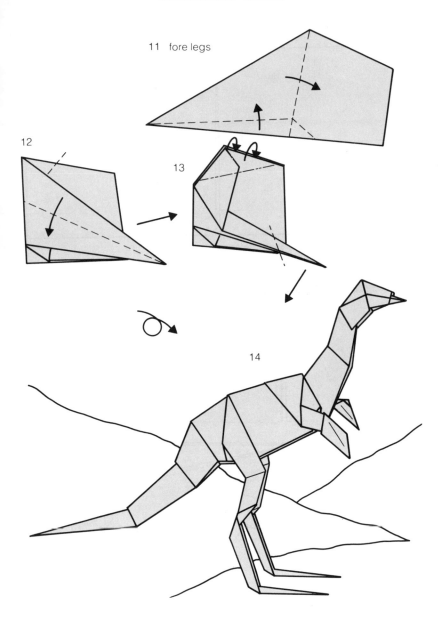

1

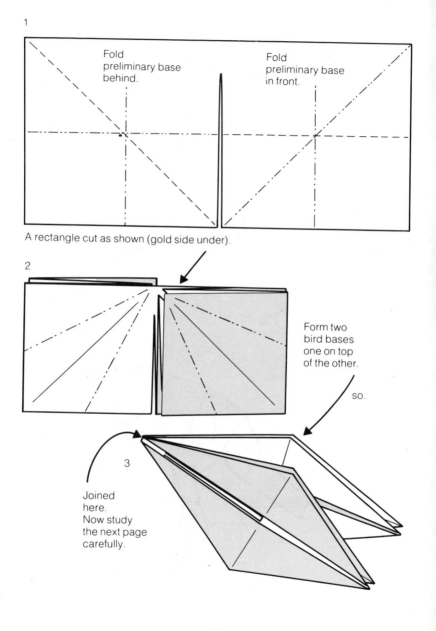

Fold preliminary base behind.

Fold preliminary base in front.

A rectangle cut as shown (gold side under).

2

Form two bird bases one on top of the other.

so.

3

Joined here. Now study the next page carefully.

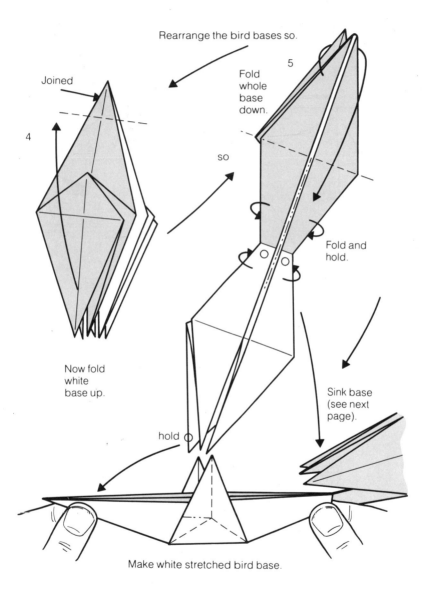

Rearrange the bird bases so.

Joined

4

5

Fold whole base down.

so

Now fold white base up.

Fold and hold.

Sink base (see next page).

hold

Make white stretched bird base.

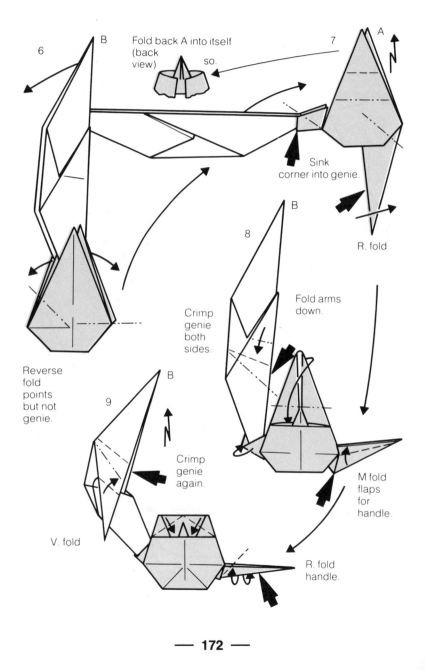

6

B

Fold back A into itself
(back
view)      so.

7

A

Sink
corner into genie.

R. fold

Reverse
fold
points
but not
genie.

B

8

Crimp
genie
both
sides.

Fold arms
down.

M fold
flaps
for
handle.

B

9

Crimp
genie
again.

V. fold

R. fold
handle.

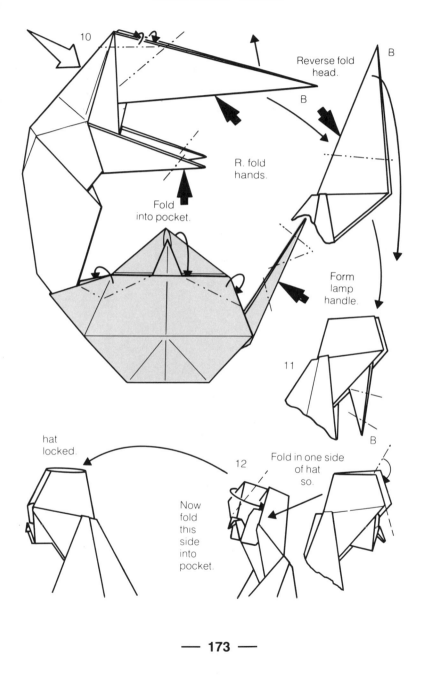

10

Reverse fold
head.

B

B

R. fold
hands.

Fold
into pocket.

Form
lamp
handle.

11

B

hat
locked.

12

Fold in one side
of hat
so.

Now
fold
this
side
into
pocket.

— **173** —

14

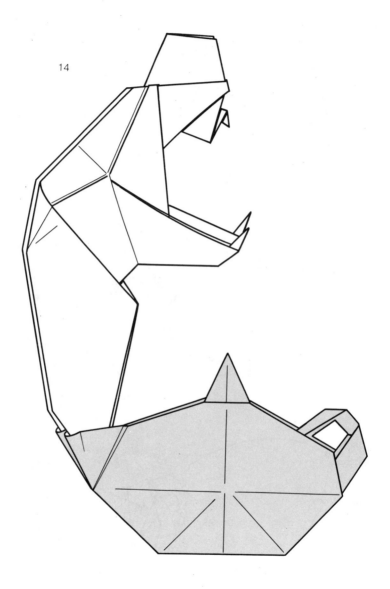

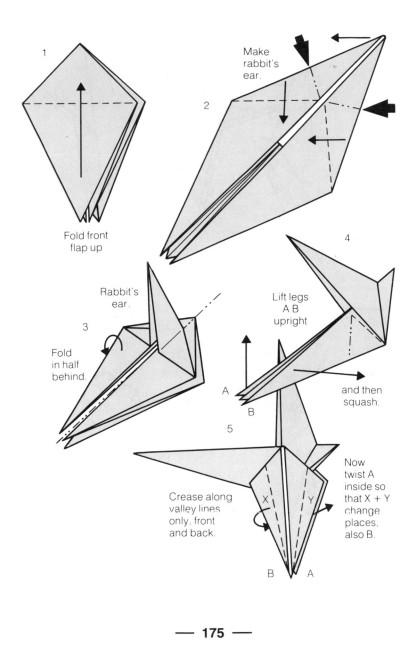

1

Fold front
flap up

2

Make
rabbit's
ear.

3

Rabbit's
ear.

Fold
in half
behind.

4

Lift legs
A B
upright

A

B

and then
squash.

5

Crease along
valley lines
only, front
and back.

X

Y

Now
twist A
inside so
that X + Y
change
places.
also B.

B    A

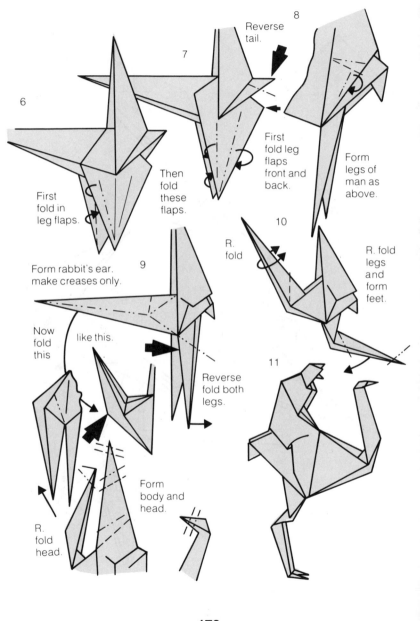

8

Reverse tail.

First fold leg flaps front and back.

Form legs of man as above.

7

6

First fold in leg flaps.

Then fold these flaps.

Form rabbit's ear. make creases only.

9

10

R. fold

R. fold legs and form feet.

Now fold this

like this.

Reverse fold both legs.

11

R. fold head.

Form body and head.

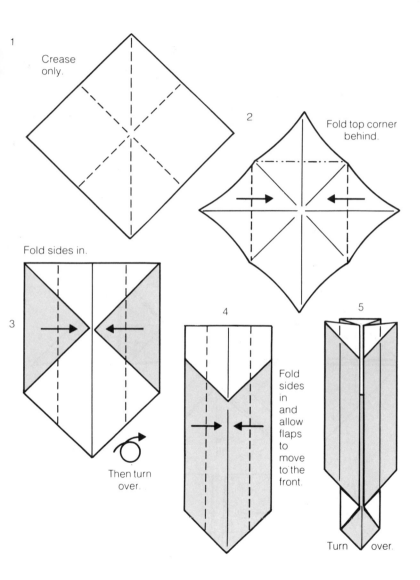

1

Crease only.

2

Fold top corner behind.

Fold sides in.

3

Then turn over.

4

Fold sides in and allow flaps to move to the front.

5

Turn over.

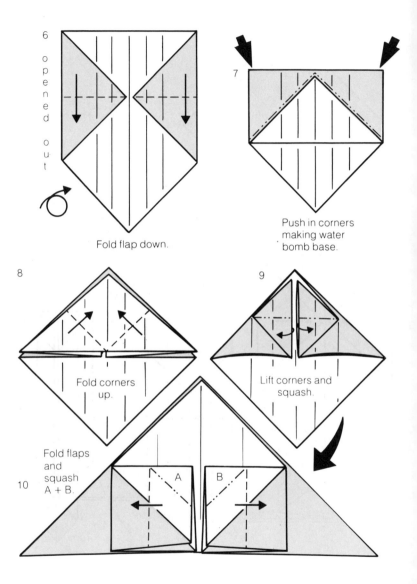

6 opened out

Fold flap down.

7 Push in corners making water bomb base.

8 Fold corners up.

9 Lift corners and squash.

10 Fold flaps and squash A + B.

A

B

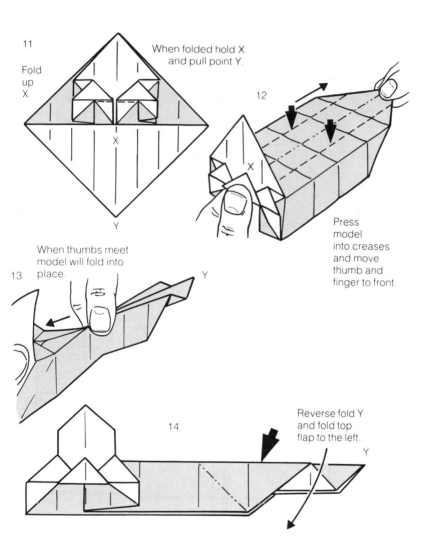

11

Fold up X.

When folded hold X and pull point Y.

12

X

Y

Press model into creases and move thumb and finger to front.

When thumbs meet model will fold into place.

13

Y

14

Reverse fold Y and fold top flap to the left.

Y

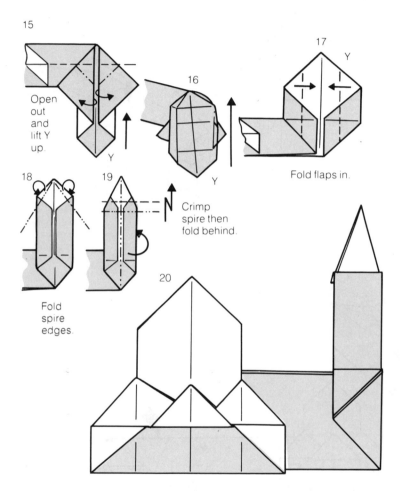

15

Open
out
and
lift Y
up.

Y

16

Y

17

Y

Fold flaps in.

18

19

Crimp
spire then
fold behind.

Fold
spire
edges.

20

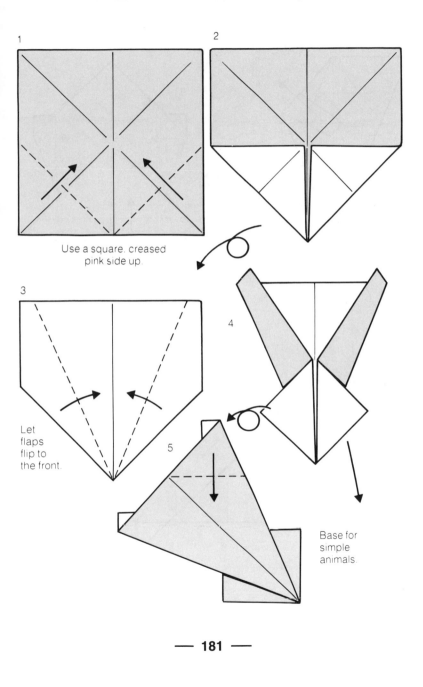

1

Use a square, creased
pink side up.

2

3

Let
flaps
flip to
the front.

4

5

Base for
simple
animals.

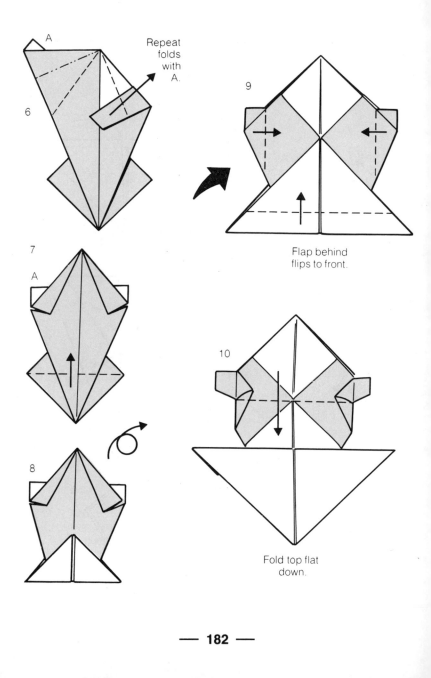

6

A

Repeat
folds
with
A.

9

Flap behind
flips to front.

7

A

8

10

Fold top flat
down.

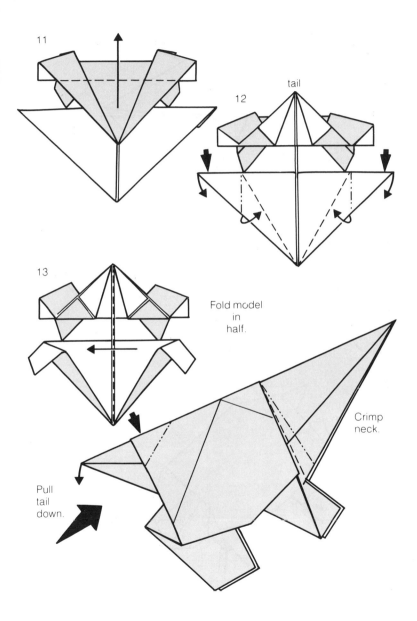

11

12

tail

13

Fold model
in
half.

Crimp
neck.

Pull
tail
down.

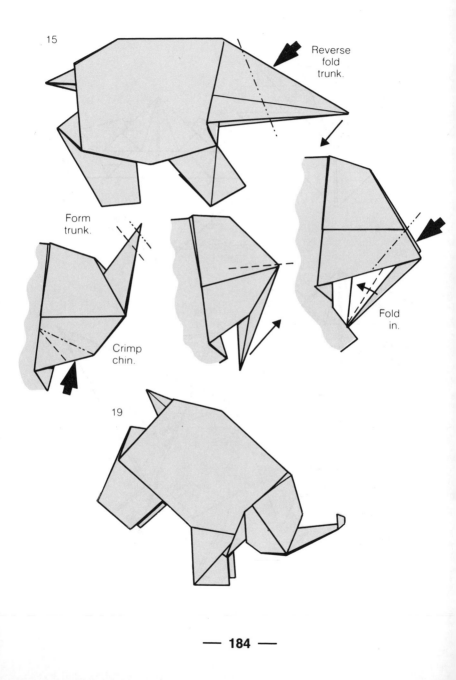

15

Reverse
fold
trunk.

Form
trunk.

Crimp
chin.

Fold
in.

19

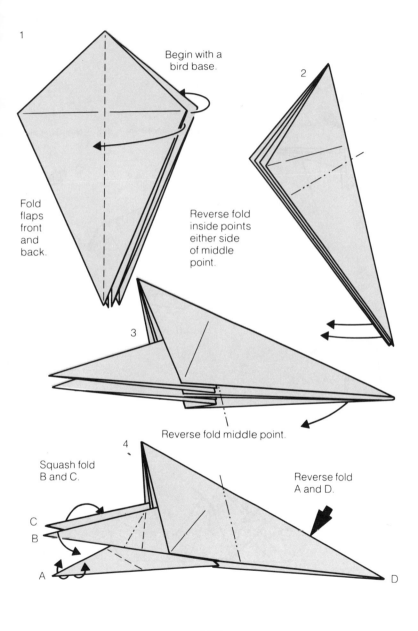

1

Begin with a bird base.

Fold flaps front and back.

2

Reverse fold inside points either side of middle point.

3

Reverse fold middle point.

4

Squash fold B and C.

Reverse fold A and D.

C

B

A

D

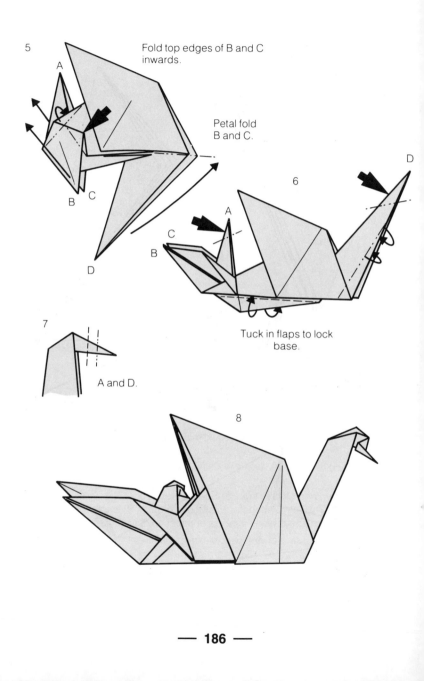

5

Fold top edges of B and C inwards.

Petal fold B and C.

6

Tuck in flaps to lock base.

7

A and D.

8

# Bibliography

by David Lister

Books about origami now number well over a thousand, but many of them are designed for children. The following books include models of a wide range of difficulty and have been selected mainly for their interest for serious folders and because they are likely to be available in bookshops or libraries.

**Kenneway, Eric**
*Simple Origami* (1970) Dryad Press, Leicester.
*Origami in action* (1972) Dryad Press, Leicester.
*Origami – Paperfolding for Fun* (1980) Octopus Books, London.
*Complete Origami* (1987) Ebury Press, London.

This last is not primarily a book of instructions, but a delightful encyclopedia of models and numerous unexpected facets of paper-folding.

**Temko, Florence**
*Paper Pandas and Jumping Frogs* (1986) China Books, San Francisco.

**Jackson, Paul**
*Origami: a Complete Step-by-Step Guide* (1989) Hamlyn, London.
*Classic Origami* (1990) Quarto Publishing, London.

**Biddle, Steve and Megumi**
*Amazing Origami for Children* (1990) Arrow Books, London.
*Step-by-Step Origami* (1991) Ebury Press, London.

Some books of American 'technical' folding:

**Montroll, John**
*Origami for the Enthusiast* (1979) Drew Publications, New York.
*Origami Sculptures* (1985) Antroll Publishing, Vermont.

**Lang, Robert J.**
*The Complete Book of Origami* (1988) Dover Publications, New York.

**Montroll, John** and **Lang, Robert J.**
Origami Sea Life (1990) Antroll Publishing, Vermont, USA.

**Engel, Peter**
*Folding the Universe* (1989) Vintage Books, New York.
(Apart from 227 pages of models, this book contains 81 pages of fascinating serious discussion about many aspects of paper-folding.)

Some books by Japanese authors available in English:

**Kawai, Toyoaki**
*Colourful Origami* (this edition 1983) Barnes and Noble, New York.

**Nakano, Dokushtei** (translated by Eric Kenneway)
*Easy Origami* (1985) Viking Kestrel, Harmondsworth.

**Takahama, Toshie**
*The Joy of Origami* (1985) Shufunotomo, Tokyo.

**Kasahara, Kunihiko**
*Origami for the Connisseur* Japan Publications, Tokyo.

**Kasahara, Kunihiko**
*Origami Omnibus* (1988) Japan Publications, Tokyo.
(This is a huge collection of every sort of paper-folding.)

Three classic works still in print:

**Murray, W. D.** and **Rigney, F. J.**
*Paper-folding for Beginners* (1928, this edition 1960) Dover Publications, New York.

**Campbell, Margaret**
*Paper Toy Making* (1937, this edition 1964) Dover Publications, New York.

**Harbin, Robert**
*Paper Magic* (1956, this edition 1971) John Maxfield, London.

The first two of these classics were the best paper-folding books published in English before Robert Harbin's *Paper Magic*. They were the books from which Lillian Oppenheimer and Robert Harbin learnt much of their folding. *Paper Magic* took their place and is still an excellent non-technical introduction to the subject.

Three more classics from the early 1960s:

**Randlett, Samuel**
*The Art of Origami* (1961) Faber and Faber, London.
*The Best of Origami* (1963) Faber and Faber, London.

**Harbin, Robert**
*Secrets of Origami* (1964) Oldborne Press, London. (Later edition Octopus Books, London.)

Robert Harbin and Samuel Randlett co-operated when writing these three books, which heralded modern paper-folding in the West. Unfortunately they are out-of-print, but they can be found in libraries and secondhand bookshops.

The Japanese output is enormous, both for children and serious folders. The British Origami Society and other paper-folding societies will advise on the best and how to obtain them. Japanese authors to look for include Akira Yoshizawa, Toshie Takahama, Toyraki Kawai, Kumihiko Kasahara, Yoshihide Momotani and Tomoko Fuse.

Language is no barrier to following an origami book because the same symbols for diagrams are used throughout the world. There are many books in Spanish, French, Dutch, German and Italian which are worth having and the origami societies will be pleased to give guidance. Some of the societies themselves issue publications which are not obtainable elsewhere.